Edward Arthur Brayley Hodgetts

Round About Armenia

The Record of a Journey Across the Balkans Through Turkey, the Caucasus, and

Persia in 1895

Edward Arthur Brayley Hodgetts

Round About Armenia

The Record of a Journey Across the Balkans Through Turkey, the Caucasus, and Persia in 1895

ISBN/EAN: 9783744753821

Printed in Europe, USA, Canada, Australia, Japan

Cover: Foto ©Andreas Hilbeck / pixelio.de

More available books at **www.hansebooks.com**

ROUND ABOUT ARMENIA

THE CATHOLICOS OF ARMENIA,

WITH ETCHMIADZIN CATHEDRAL AND MOUNT ARARAT IN THE BACKGROUND.

From a Photograph by the Monks of Etchmiadzin.

ROUND ABOUT ARMENIA

THE RECORD OF A JOURNEY ACROSS THE BALKANS

THROUGH TURKEY, THE CAUCASUS,

AND PERSIA IN

1895

BY

E. A. BRAYLEY HODGETTS

AUTHOR OF "IN THE TRACK OF THE RUSSIAN FAMINE," ETC.

LONDON

SAMPSON LOW, MARSTON AND COMPANY

LIMITED

St. Dunstan's House

FETTER LANE, FLEET STREET, E.C.

1896

LONDON :

PRINTED BY WILLIAM CLOWES AND SONS, LIMITED,

STAMFORD STREET AND CHARING CROSS.

PREFACE.

THE book herewith offered to the public is in no
sense a reprint of the letters which appeared in the
Daily Graphic in the first half of last year, but is a
consecutive record of my travels in the East in 1895,
written in the light of the most recent events.

In this record I have laboured rather to explain the
causes which have brought about the present state of
affairs in Asia Minor, than to excite the passions of
the reader by a recital of the repulsive details of
cruelty which attended the massacres. Those details
are unfit for publication, and, in my opinion, unless it
is possible to publish a full and exhaustive body of
evidence, it is better to limit the statement to general
terms. Besides, the Blue Books have already made
accessible to the public a sufficiently blood-curdling
series of authentic " atrocities."

The objection may be raised that as my journey
was undertaken in the first half of 1895, the wholesale
massacres with which Asia Minor was visited since
then could not have come under my observation, and

that, therefore, the present book belongs to a chapter of the ancient history of the Armenian Question, but cannot pretend to take in the entire situation. With this view I may be permitted to disagree. The tactics of the ruling Powers of Turkey have not altered, the policy remains the same, and, notwithstanding the popular outbreak in Constantinople, which the Ambassadors to the Porte themselves asserted in their Collective Note was carefully planned at Yildiz Kiosk, the situation is stationary, except that the massacre of a few thousand Armenians in the streets of Constantinople seems to have excited English public opinion far more than the nameless horrors perpetrated over the entire extent of Turkish Armenia.

In the *Pall Mall Gazette* for January 14th, 1896, I summed up, in an article entitled "The Revolutionary Movement in Armenia," the state of affairs in the following words :—

"Turkey, egged on by Russia, has been wiping out the Armenians in order to suppress the revolutionary movement, which has been fed by Russian Armenians, and with Armenian gold. . . . By thus wiping out the Armenians in her traditional manner, she has brought her own disintegration within visible distance, and Russia, posing as the friend of peace, the protector of Christians, and the great humanitarian Power of Eastern Europe, is quietly sitting down, pretending to help both Europe and Turkey, but really obstructing them all, and calmly waiting for the fulness of time when Turkey will fall to pieces, and she will pick up the fragments. In the meantime, the Armenians, who wanted to found an independent Armenia, are being massacred, and perfidious England gets all the blame; while Germany and Austria, fearful of opening up the Eastern Question, are backing up Russian diplomacy. Verily Prince Lobanoff-Rostovski is a second Bismarck. But the end is not yet, and what that end will be depends upon so many factors that he would be a bold man who would venture on a prophecy."

Nothing has happened since those words were written to alter my view of the situation. In my opinion, the duty and interests of England are clear, and I am glad to see that such authorities as Canon MacColl and Mr. James Bryce, M.P., seem to share my sentiments. Mr. Bryce, who is perhaps at once one of the greatest living authorities on International Law and on Armenia, said, in a letter read at the Corn Exchange Meeting at Oxford, and published in the *Times* for September 25th, 1896 :—

"Do not let us assume that the action of Britain is confronted by the risk of European war. The documents bearing on the question, so far as they are known to us, supply no sufficient ground for this assumption, and the real danger to the peace of Europe seems rather to lie in a continuance of the reign of terror in Constantinople and Asia Minor, which must ultimately bring about the interference of some at least of the Powers under circumstances far more likely to lead to a conflict than would the removal from the throne he has disgraced of the author of these misdeeds."

That is pretty plain language. Those who still

place their faith in Russia should read Lord Robert
Montagu's interesting book on " The Eastern Question," published in 1877 by Messrs. Chapman and
Hall, in which a masterly picture of the policy of
Russia is presented, and where the author illustrates,
by extracts from the despatches of our Ambassador
to the Court of St. Petersburg, Lord Augustus Loftus,
what sort of treatment the Armenians may expect
from the benignant rule of Russia. The atrocities
committed by the Cossacks on the Uniate Greek
Catholics of Poland were only one degree less horrible
than those perpetrated in the name of the Sultan
upon the Armenians.

We are going through a critical period in our
history, for there is a general tendency among the
Powers to hustle us at every turn, whether with the
object of forcing us to join one or the other of the
opposing camps of European politics, as some suppose,
or simply with the view to weakening us, as I think
more probable, does not signify. I believe that, if we
do not actively intervene in Turkey, we shall presently
find the diplomatical chess-board so disposed that we
shall be at a great disadvantage. The examples of
Siam, China, and Madagascar are not alarming, but
they are significant.

On October 31st, 1895, *Vanity Fair* published an
article in which I said :—

"Whatever happens there can be little doubt that we are,
diplomatically, in hot water everywhere. At this juncture,

especially after the Armenian fiasco, it would be well for us to take to heart the advice of Polonius to Laertes : ' Beware of entrance to a quarrel ; but, being in, bear it, that the opposer may beware of thee.' For the rest we have been in the same predicament before, especially at the beginning of the present century. Curiously enough, these periods have synchronised with those of our greatness."

I do not think that our international position has improved since the above was written, and I fail to see what object can be served by holding public meetings to denounce the Sultan if we always make it clear that nothing will induce us to take independent and active steps to translate our sentiments into acts.

We have lived at peace with all the world for so long that it is difficult for us to bring ourselves to face, in any other than an academic attitude, the possible contingency of having to fight for our national existence, to say nothing of our Empire. But it would seem that that contingency is not so remote as some people suppose.

I have appended to this book the best map of Armenia that I could find, and I hope the reader will agree in pronouncing it to be excellent ; yet it fails to indicate all the places where massacres have occurred. I have, however, marked in red a sufficient number to give a fairly good general idea of the area over which they have extended.

A word about the Armenians themselves. These much abused people, although undoubtedly sharing in the vices common to oppressed nationalities, struck me in the main as being a fine, sturdy, and industrious race, who, under favourable conditions, could develop into a respectable and vigorous nation.

E. A. Brayley Hodgetts.

39, Redcliffe Square,
    South Kensington,
        September, 1896.

CONTENTS.

CHAP.   PAGE

I.—SOFIA AND CONSTANTINOPLE . . . 1

II.—THE BLACK SEA TO TREBIZOND . 24

III.—TIFLIS, THE QUEEN OF THE CAUCASUS . 43

IV.—THE STATE OF PARTIES IN RUSSIAN
ARMENIA 62

V.—THE SASSUN MASSACRES 85

VI.—RESOURCES AND ECONOMIC CONDITION OF
TURKISH ARMENIA 113

VII.—SOCIAL AMENITIES 135

VIII.—BAKU 147

IX.—ACROSS THE CASPIAN TO RESHT 167

X.—ON HORSEBACK TO TABREEZ . 189

XI.—TABREEZ TO ERIVAN . . . 208

XII.—ETCHMIADZIN 226

XIII.—THE RUSSIAN SHORES OF THE BLACK SEA. 245

XIV.—THE ARMENIAN QUESTION . . . 266

INDEX 291

ROUND ABOUT ARMENIA.

CHAPTER I.

SOFIA AND CONSTANTINOPLE.

It was in the January of 1895 that I started, for the *Daily Graphic*, on a journey of investigation into the Armenian atrocities. It was my first visit to the East. Russia I knew well, I had travelled over the principal countries of Europe, and had been as far west as New York; but I felt that until I had seen Constantinople I could not pretend to know anything about the world.

It was therefore with a feeling of more than ordinary excitement and anticipation that I took my seat in the train which was to whirl me direct to the capital of the Osmanli.

For equipment for my mission I had two general ideas. One developed out of my inner consciousness, the other obtained from a friend in London who had special means of hearing the views of the ruling powers in Turkey. For the sake of convenience

I will state my friend's theory of the massacres before giving my own.

He said in the first place that there had been no massacres at all, and in the second that the disturbances had arisen out of some disputes between Kurds and Armenians, which the Turks had put down with some severity, and that that was all there was to be said.

The theory I had evolved out of my inner consciousness was equally simple. It was that history was repeating itself, and that we were on the eve of the enfranchisement of Armenia. The dissolution of the Turkish Empire has been going on piecemeal for the last century or so by provinces. Each province falls away from Turkey very much on the following lines. First, there is a revolutionary movement, then there are massacres, which enlist the sympathy of Europe. These are succeeded by an organised rebellion ; the rebels are assisted by foreign volunteers, and generally obtain their independence. It was more or less on these lines that the independence of Greece and of the many states of the Balkan peninsula has been achieved, and I thought that we had before us once more a similar national movement.

Looking back upon all I have seen, heard, and read, I am now inclined to believe that, after all, my own theory was not so far out. According to this theory of course it would be necessary to assume that the massacres were provoked by designing persons, whose object it was to excite the indignation of European public opinion against the Turks. Emancipators are usually rather careless about spilling the blood of the people they wish to emancipate. One historical axiom it is well to bear in mind—whenever Turkey is about to lose a province she first massacres the population.

As we go on, however, we shall see that general ideas, excellent as they are, are apt to be complicated with special ideas, and that the situation in Armenia is not quite so simple or so easy of comprehension as would at first appear.

Having stated my general idea, the reader will not be surprised to learn that I determined to make a halt at Sofia on my way to Constantinople, to endeavour to ascertain there whether there was not going on simultaneously with the Armenian movement a Macedonian movement.

Subsequent events have shown that I was not mistaken in my surmise, but I had omitted several factors from my calculation. One was the appointment of Prince Lobanoff Rostovski to the Chancellorship of the Russian Empire, and the return by him to the old active policy of Russia. I knew Prince Lobanoff Rostovski was going to succeed M. de Giers, and I knew that he was one of the ablest diplomatists and statesmen Russia possessed ; but even so I find I underrated his ability. He has proved more than a match for the whole of Europe. The other factor

was the murder of Stambuloff and the consequences
of that disaster on the political attitude of Bulgaria.
That Stambuloff was a doomed man everybody knew,
and nobody better than Stambuloff himself, but that
Bulgaria should after his death have thrown itself
without reservation into the arms of Russia, even
M. Stoïloff did not suspect at the time. These
two factors have altered the course of events. Had
Macedonia risen, as was intended, Turkey would have
had her hands full, and Russia could not have inter-
fered to help her in Armenia. All this is now
changed, for the moment at least, though we may
yet see another turn in the kaleidoscope of continental
politics.

One thing seems to be certain, the Powers appear
to have made up their minds that the lives of a few
thousand Armenians, more or less, are not worth
incurring the risk of a European war. But this is not
the first time that the Powers have tried to prevent a
war over the Eastern question ; nevertheless, they
have not been invariably successful.

The train which took me to Vienna was represented
to me as a through train from Ostend to Constantinople. It was nothing of the kind. It went to
Vienna directly enough, but there it stopped, and
I had to get out and take my chance of getting a
berth in the Oriental express from Paris. This is
a grievous inconvenience, and travellers should be
warned against it.

The train was certainly very luxurious, and went through beautiful scenery. On board I met a British artillery officer, who was going on leave of absence to Egypt. Hearing that I was going to Armenia, he asked me to allow him to accompany me, and I accepted his offer with pleasure. I shall have more to say of him presently.

The Sofia station is several miles from the town of that name, and I was driven in an open carriage drawn by two horses along a road which was covered with mud about a foot deep. In this conveyance I was taken to the only hotel which Sofia boasts, the Hôtel Bulgaria. It was fairly clean, roomy, and comfortable, but the food was execrable. The police regulations were easy, I was not bothered about my passport.

Sofia is little better than a village, it is a sort of Slough of Despond, surrounded by hills, and paved, like the road to another place, with good intentions, and nothing else. There are one or two houses in this curious capital of the peasant state which look as though they might have belonged to the outermost outskirts of Berlin or even Paris, but with these exceptions, and the really pretty palace of the Prince, the handsome public park, and a few villas, the town of Sofia is not unlike the town of Trebizond, or any other third-rate Turkish city.

To me it was strangely suggestive of Thackeray's celebrated Pumpernickel. There was an air of un- reality about everything. The bodyguard of the

Prince is composed of a squadron of hussars without horses. The Prime Minister presides over a Council of Ministers composed principally of himself. At the time I was at Sofia he was Minister of the Interior, Minister of Finance, and half a dozen other Ministers all rolled into one. The Prince's private secretary has some tremendous high-sounding office, that of Chief of Chancellerie, I believe, and everybody has a title ; all educated Bulgarians are doctors.

But if the state and pomp of the little peasant principality seem somewhat like that of the Grand Duchy of Geroldstein, the army is not an army *pour rire* at all, but a very serious body. A nation under arms must be serious, but when that nation is composed of hardy peasants, and the soldiers average six feet in their stockings, and are broad shouldered and well set up, it is most impressive. As there is no aristocracy in Bulgaria, the officers are peasants too, and fine men they are, dignified and workman-like, thoroughly smart and soldierly, but without the least vestige of swagger. I had seen some Servian troops on my journey through that country, and was much struck by the contrast between them and the Bulgarians. The Servians I saw were a slouching untidy lot, not to be compared with the quiet earnest Bulgarians. During my stay at Sofia I had the good fortune to see a review, and I was astounded at the precision and smartness of the men. They marched better than German or Russian troops.

Thus the first impression produced upon the mind by Sofia is comic. You see the gorgeous princely palace in this desert of mud, the smart sentries and the smart officers rubbing shoulders with slovenly dirty peasants in a slovenly dirty village, and you feel inclined to laugh. But you look up at the frowning snow-clad Balkans towering over you, and down again upon the earnest simple faces of these soldiers and peasants, and you feel that this is no swaggering burlesque, but very serious real life. These men have fought for their independence ; they have spent their blood and their hard-earned coin to get their freedom, and they are terribly in earnest. That is indeed the whole secret of Bulgarian independence —everybody is in grim earnest. The Bulgarians do not care about amusements. Sofia has no theatres, only cafés. The principal articles of merchandise seem to be newspapers and revolvers. The papers are not filled with gossip and chit-chat, but are deadly serious, so are the people in the cafés who discuss them. It is not safe to contradict a Bulgarian. Another peculiarity of Sofia is that you see no old men there. I only saw one myself, and I am per- suaded that he was an accident. . The tradespeople are mostly Austrians, and the fathers of the young men who are serving their country, or making history at the Sobranye, are minding their farms.

During the few days that I stayed at Sofia I saw Dr. Stoïloff, Mr. Stambuloff, Sir Arthur Nicolson, and

many other notabilities. Prince Ferdinand refused
to see me, because he had ascertained that I had
previously called on Sir Arthur Nicolson, whose
children were down with chicken-pox, and the health
of Prince Boris is guarded with almost superstitious
care.   Dr. Stoïloff, who spoke English perfectly,
impressed me very favourably.   He was full of fiscal
reforms.   With regard to Russia, he gave me to
understand that Bulgaria had no intention of reviving
the days of the Russian occupation, and did not
intend to make concessions to Russia without receiving something in return.   Prince Ferdinand's private
secretary expressed himself very much to the same
effect, and said that Bulgarians were "Slavs" and
long-headed.

My visit to Stambuloff was surrounded with a
certain atmosphere of romance.   In the first place, it
was not easy to get admission.   I rang the bell at the
door of his low and simple dwelling, but it was some
time before it was answered, and even then his
servant would not let me in, but demanded my
business, took my card, and slammed the door in my
face.   I waited fully five minutes on the doorstep
before I was admitted.   Finally I was ushered into
Stambuloff's sanctum, which looked more like an
armoury than a study, so well provided was it with
revolvers and guns.

Stambuloff received me with much simplicity of
manner.   Not tall in stature, he had a face disfigured

by a pair of black and straight bushy eyebrows, and a frown like that of Ivan the Terrible. His face was pale, rather soft and plump about the cheeks, and he had most uncanny black eyes. I had never seen eyes like his before. They looked absolutely small, leaden, and dead, and then they could flash out bright and glowing, full of life and passion, and of genius. But there was something secretive and reserved about Stambuloff, though he spoke frankly enough to me. In all he said I felt that he was scrupulously honest, and even morbidly afraid of influencing me by the angry passions which I could see surging up in his nervous face. I could not help feeling, as I talked to him and heard him talk, that his mind was like a seething cauldron, but unfathomable. From Stambuloff I gathered that the annexation of Macedonia was but a question of time, and from my conversations with the various gentlemen I named I arrived at the following conclusions.

Bulgaria has no industries and no capital, and is groaning under excessive taxation. Owing to the capitalisation treaties with Turkey, Bulgaria, which is a vassal state of Turkey, is hopelessly handicapped by Austria. Austrian trade in Eastern Europe is a very much more important factor than we in England perhaps think. At present Bulgaria is in the hands of Austria. Her alternative is to throw herself into the arms of Russia. In order to maintain a large and magnificent army, Bulgaria is being slowly ruined.

There is only one way of averting this ruin, that is by conquest. It is no use blinking this question. But conquest of what? Well, Macedonia. That will mean the enmity of Greece and Servia. Of course if Bulgaria could have carried out Stambuloff's idea and formed a sort of triple alliance with Turkey and Roumania, all might have been well ; she would have been able to snap her fingers at Greece and Servia, and even escape from the upper and nether millstones of Russia and Austria. But that was not to be. The affairs of Bulgaria have fallen out of the iron hand of Stambuloff into the supple grasp of Prince Ferdinand, whose one ambition is to become a recognised ruler. Whether that ambition will be gratified for long remains to be seen.

The present situation in Bulgaria is therefore briefly this : Here is a peasant population, surrounded by enemies, which has maintained itself, armed to the teeth, in spite of its foes, who are now, however, sapping its vitals. The country imports all manufactured articles, and must pay for them with corn, wine, and cattle. But both Russia and Austria are agricultural as well as industrial countries, and it does not therefore signify greatly to Bulgaria whether she is exploited by one or the other. What is of consequence is that to-day the markets of the world are already glutted with agricultural produce. A peaceful solution of Bulgaria's impulse is practically impossible, and my own opinion is that Bulgaria will either become a Russian province, which does not seem probable, or will have to fight for her existence. If she adopts the latter policy I believe that she will come out strong, and may become the Prussia of the Balkans. This I shrewdly suspect Stambuloff saw. He would have secured the friendship of Austria, and defied Russia. With the Armenian rebellion in one corner of her dominions, and a Macedonian rising in the other, Turkey would have been helpless ; but Stambuloff is no more, the political cards have been shuffled, and Russia holds all the trumps. I do not think, however, that the English people need take more than a platonic interest in the Balkans. Some time or other there will be a disturbance of the centre of gravity in those regions, but for the present at least that time seems to have been postponed indefinitely. Several friends of mine have told me that in the view I take of the condition of Bulgaria I am prejudiced, and that there is no reason whatever why that country should not gently and peacefully develop. They may be right, at the same time I must be allowed to retain my prejudices.

Equipped with these prejudices, hastily acquired, I went off to Constantinople. I will not dwell upon the amusing experiences that I had on the Turkish frontier. My own passport was in perfect order, but in the same train there was an unfortunate French engineer, who had no passport at all, and who further excited the suspicions of the Turkish custom-house

authorities, by a very curious apparatus, which turned
out to be a photographic camera, and a couple of
mysterious boxes, which contained plates. These
plates he had to expose to the rude and puzzled gaze
of the ingenuous Turks ; but I am afraid I do not
remember his fate. Whether he was cruelly tortured
in a dark dungeon, or sewn up in a sack and thrown
into the Bosphorus, I am quite unable to say. On
board the train I received a very curious indication of
the way the wind was blowing in Germany. Among
the passengers was a German lawyer attached to the
German Embassy at Constantinople, and this gentleman on one occasion, while the conversation was
turning on the subject of the Armenian massacres,
expressed his compassion for the Sultan and the
unfortunate Turks, who were being so unjustly
calumniated and ill-treated.

"The poor Turk !" he said, with much dignity, " he
is so courteous and charming and amiable ; it really
is wicked that he should be thus persecuted and made
the subject of horrible accusations and political
intrigues !"

I had hitherto rather stupidly supposed that the
Armenian was the person who was being persecuted,
but it is wonderful how the mind is enlarged by
travel.

On my arrival at Constantinople, in which capital
by the bye I was much disappointed, I met my friend
the artillery officer who had preceded me, and put

up at the right hotel, opened the campaign at the Embassy for me, and had actually bought a map of Armenia in the Grande Rue de Péra. I afterwards discovered that the same map had been prohibited in Russia, and when I wanted to get another copy at Tiflis, I found that no shopkeeper could supply it. One of the first people I met in Constantinople was a gentleman, who told me he belonged to the young Turkey party. His general views are so interesting that I think I cannot do better than state them here, especially as I discovered later that this gentleman was a person of considerable political importance. I will not do him the bad service of revealing his name, especially as I do not know whether he has escaped imprisonment or not.

In the first place he informed me, what has since been corroborated by events, that Turkey was honey-combed with revolutionary societies, but that there was very little cohesion amongst them. "What is sucking the vitals of Turkey," he said, "is polygamy. Many of our young men recognise this, and do not have more than one wife. But even so the women are stupid and uneducated. We want in Turkey clever, well-educated women to be the mothers of our children, and to bring up a race which shall revolt against the iniquities of the present *régime*. The subjugation of woman is the great curse of Turkey. As long as the present family-life and general structure of society continues in Turkey we shall go from bad to worse. There is nothing to save us. The government is rotten. Those whom the Sultan distrusts or who have disgraced themselves, but who are too powerful to be punished, he makes governors of distant provinces. The Sultan is absolutely wicked. He has no sense of patriotism, no feeling of justice or honesty. Do you know that he spends millions a year on the press of Europe, in order to humbug and bamboozle public opinion? But he allows his fleet to rot. Do you know why? He is afraid that those very vessels might be used against him. He trusts nobody. His great fear is assassination. He lives in terror of that all his days. His great passion is avarice. He hoards and hoards, and all for no reason, with no object. He is a miserable creature, with a weak constitution, delicate chest, and a low type of mind; but he is very cunning. Some day or other, however, he will be murdered, we shall have a revolution, and then Turkey will revive. The Turks are not played out yet. They are a fine race, and they have plenty of reserve force."

With regard to the Armenian massacres his views were equally sharp and well-defined.

"How," said he, "could the Armenian survivors of the massacres have written the letters which have appeared in the press? Those survivors are supposed to be illiterate peasants. As a matter of fact, I know that the letters were written in London in the rooms of the agitators, they never came from Sassun! What really happened was this. The Kurds and Armenians live in scattered villages, and there is no dividing line to show where the Kurds leave off and the Armenians begin. But the Kurds being Mahomedans, and the Armenians Christians, conflicts continually arise between the two races. Sometimes, of course, these conflicts assume larger proportions than usual, and it is necessary for the Turkish troops to come and establish order. This is what has happened at Sassun. The Kurds and Armenians have had a more than usually severe tussle, and so the governor of the district sent troops to quell the disorders. When these troops arrived at Sassun they found the Armenians drawn up to receive them, for they mistook them for Kurds. The Turkish troops, on the other hand, thinking the Armenians had turned out to resist them, opened fire on them, and thus a fight was precipitated, in which women and children were shot down as well as men ; but then the women were armed. Out there the women are quite as good fighters as the men."

It is quite unnecessary to make any comments on these statements. I have little doubt that, as a general review of the condition of things in Armenia, my informant was for a Turk fairly impartial ; but as I have already hinted, the Armenian question is too intricate and too large to be settled off hand in a few glib sentences.

The father of my friend, the artillery officer, had

been engaged years ago upon the construction of the great arsenal at Constantinople, the Top-hané, and the son was naturally very anxious to view it. He therefore made application to the Grand Master of the Ordnance, Zekki Pasha, and took me with him. It was a most interesting visit. In the first place, I must in fairness admit that Stamboul is a much finer city than Pera. The streets are broad and clean, the air is pure, and the people look dignified and decent. This cannot be said of the European city of Pera, which is a dirty, dingy, disgusting collection of defilement. The Grande Rue de Péra is for the best part of its length narrow and filthy, with few shops, but no pavements. Still Pera is an interesting place, on account of the wonderful variety of national costume which one meets in the streets ; and the view from the hill, where the principal hotels are, into the Golden Horn is really beautiful. For all that, Pera is not the city of all others in which I should like to settle down and spend my days. Besides, of recent years it has become dull and monotonous ; there is a theatre for Greek and Armenian plays, and a circus, and a very vile *café chantant*, but beyond this there are no amusements. There is scarcely a provincial town in Russia which is not a more agreeable place to live in.

The Top-hané is situated in Galata, and is therefore half way between Stamboul and Pera. It is a surprising place. The enormous entrance hall, to get to which a dirty but spacious courtyard had to be traversed, looked very much like a big stable. In it were standing horses and carriages of all descriptions, and there was a perpetual flow of persons coming to see the officials. Many of these were English mechanics, decked out in the uniform of the Turkish army, and holding the rank of colonels and generals. What struck me most about all the people was their shortness of stature, and the slightness of build of the younger men. Of course the older Turks were very portly and podgy, but they were all small and weak looking. Even the Englishmen were slight and short, but they could be easily distinguished from the Turks by reason of their fair complexion, clear blue eyes, neat figures, and general smartness. We ascended a broad wooden staircase, at the top of which we were stopped by a sentry, and we had to send a dragoman inside to explain our business before we were admitted. These dragomans seem to know everybody, and to have the open sesamé everywhere. They are generally in the pay of the police, and those who are not thieves and scoundrels are spies. Some combine the two functions.

At length we were ushered into a long low room, badly lighted, the walls whitewashed, and the general appearance anything but prepossessing. Here we were kept waiting some time, and presently were escorted by a smart young aide-de-camp, very beautiful to look upon, and covered with gold lace,

C

into the presence of Zekki Pasha. His office was
furnished like a Russian drawing-room. In the
centre of the room, which was very large and airy,
stood a handsome writing-table, commodious and
elegant. Round this were placed a number of very
ordinary armchairs covered with some cheap kind of
red silk. The floor was handsomely carpeted.

Zekki Pasha is a quaint little man, with a fat
round back, a fat paunch, a hook nose, grey beard,
and spectacles. He received us with true Oriental
politeness, and spoke French, German, and English
perfectly. I learned later that he had been the tutor
of one of the Imperial Princes, and was in great
favour with the Sultan. He told my friend that he
must ask his master the Sultan for permission to let
him see the arsenal. Then coffee was served in
Turkish fashion with cigarettes, on a tawdry Russian
tray, and thereupon, without any warning, Zekki Pasha
began discoursing on the Armenian question.

His views were as quaint as he was himself. He
explained to us that Turks were not fanatics, and
that all educated men, no matter what their nationality, had the same religion. I suppose he meant
that they had none at all. He said that a ruler had
the right to punish refractory subjects, and that the
Armenians had revolted against their ruler, and had
therefore been punished. The right of punishment
was accorded to the ruler of every civilised country.
It was a mistake to suppose that the Armenians were

a separate race. They were of no nationality. In Constantinople there were 200,000 Armenians among the population ; but the Armenians were a sect, not a nation. They were tolerated, and enjoyed perfect religious freedom. He thought it was unwise of England to quarrel with an old friend like Turkey about questions that did not really concern her, and expressed his opinion that such a policy was rash and imprudent.

While he was speaking fresh visitors kept coming in and sitting down to await their turn. I felt very much as though I was in the open market-place, and not in the private office of the chief of a great Government department ; but I must say that I was glad when I got out of the place and found myself safe and sound in my hotel within a stone's throw of the British Embassy. The next day an English officer in the Turkish service, who had relatives who were artificers at Woolwich—he himself was a colonel— brought my friend the permission of the Sultan to see the arsenal.

This little fact alone indicates how hard the Sultan works, and how he enters personally into every trifling detail connected with the management of the great and little affairs of his Empire.

While on the subject of the Turkish army, I may here note down a few observations. What very much astonished me was to see that the historic fez was rapidly giving way to a head-dress very similar to that of the Russian Cossacks, and that, generally, the Turkish uniform was being assimilated as much as possible to that of Russia. A straw will show which way the wind blows! I had heard a great deal of the magnificent Turkish soldiery, and was surprised to find the Turkish soldier a slouching, dirty, badly set-up weedy-looking creature. The men stoop when they march, and look half-starved and sickly. But it is not always the showiest horse which can do the most work, and stand the most hardships, and, after all, men are very much like horses, so that it is not safe to jump at conclusions from appearances. Nevertheless, I never saw a more miserable and utterly despicable set of men than the Turkish soldiers.

At the British Embassy Sir Philip Currie received me with that dignified urbanity for which he is distinguished, and expressed his concern at the discomforts that were in store for me. Among the *attachés* the feeling that seemed to prevail was briefly this: Armenians were reported to have been massacred. Was this true? If it was true, then it did not signify whether their numbers were represented by tens, hundreds, or thousands, or whether they had been tortured and brutally ill-used as well. The massacre of peasantry, no matter in what numbers, or how executed, was in itself a disgrace to civilisation, and was not to be tolerated. This view, I take it, is that which must be ultimately adopted by every right-minded Englishman. The details and the horrors are of no importance ; they can be elaborated in Fleet Street, for there is nobody who can come forward as an impartial eye-witness and contradict them. But the massacres are a fact, about which there can to-day be no doubt, and as such they are also a disgrace. Whether it is reasonable to expect Turkey to behave in harmony with the latest ideas of modern enlightened humanity is a very different question.

Interesting as all the views I had hitherto heard no doubt were, they did not come from unbiassed sources, and, in order to get a side-light thrown on the situation from an impartial authority totally uninterested in the deep political game which I felt certain was going on underneath, I traced my steps to the Legation of the United States and introduced myself to Mr. Terrell, the American Minister. That gentleman I found to possess a strong bias in favour of the Sultan. Of course it is unnecessary to explain what large social interests America has in Turkey. Her missionary enterprise and missionary colleges are deservedly famous. I had therefore expected a more sympathetic attitude towards the Armenians from Mr. Terrell. But he told me that he had lived many years in Constantinople, that he had the greatest personal regard for the Sultan, with whom he was on exceptionally pleasant terms, and that he felt sorry for him. The Armenians, he said, were a bad, intriguing lot, and had for years been plotting and planning rebellion against Turkey. He said there

were Armenian revolutionary societies all over
America, in London, at Marseilles, at Geneva, in
Italy, Greece, and Bulgaria ; that they were hand
and glove with the Nihilists of Russia. These massacres were, he believed, the results of a deep-laid plot,
and of a revolutionary movement that had extended
over years. He did not believe in the atrocities.
They were all lies invented by malignant Armenians
in London and elsewhere. He had himself good
reason to know what was going on in Armenia. One
of the favourite devices of the Armenian revolutionaries was to emigrate to America, become American
citizens, and then return to Armenian in order to
spread sedition and incite to rebellion. When the
Turkish authorities arrested them, they claimed the
protection of the United States, until the American
Government had been compelled to refuse to interfere
on their behalf.

I will not attempt to conceal from the reader that
the recital of all these indictments against the Armenians, tended rather to excite my pity for, than
any detestation of, them. I felt that these poor
Armenians, in their struggle for freedom, were cold-
shouldered by everybody, and that even the great and
glorious land of freedom refused to have anything to
say to them.

Thus it will be seen that the views in Constantinople were conflicting and puzzling, but through them
all I seemed to get glimpses of the truth, and these

glimpses only served to strengthen me in the original opinion which I had formed on undertaking my journey.

I had, however, no intention of remaining in Constantinople, which I soon saw was but the bazaar in which all kinds of rumours, some of the wildest, were focussed ; and so, without wasting much time or even calling on the Armenian Archbishop, I made preparations for my journey.

A brother correspondent came to me with an elaborate plan in which he asked me to join, but this I declined for many reasons, and proceeded to have my passport viséd for Erzeroum, the capital of Armenia. Once there I felt certain that I should be able to get further. I was assured that I would not be allowed to proceed thither, but, nothing daunted, I took out my *teskeré*, or Turkish travelling permit, and started, accompanied by my friend, for Trebizond on board one of the little Austrian-Lloyd steamers which ply on the Black Sea.

CHAPTER II.

THE BLACK SEA TO TREBIZOND.

GETTING into Constantinople is much easier than leaving it. My passport and my luggage were carefully examined at the custom-house before I was allowed to get into the caïque which was to take me to my steamer. People talk of the romance of being rowed about in a caïque; but it is sad to have to relate that much of this romance, so attractive at a distance, fades utterly when one is on the spot. The caïques are dirty and uncomfortable, and the boatmen are clumsy. Once or twice on our way to the steamer the boatman managed to get the caïque nearly swamped with the waves from the wash of passing tugs. Just as we thought we had got safely to the steamer we were stopped by a police caïque, and had once more to show our *teskerés*. At last we got on board the steamer, a dirty little boat, but even that was infested with police. There was a gendarme officer of the guard on board, who was going somewhere, and an official besides, who had charge of a number of peasants, whom he was taking to a port in the Black Sea, and these two important personages had small levées of friends who had come to see them off. As the Mahomedan religion does not approve of wine, these pious Turks were drinking each other's healths in bottled beer!

We did not get well off before nightfall, and therefore much of the beautiful scenery of the Bosphorus was obscured; but it was a curious sensation steaming along midway between Europe and Asia, and to see the green lights of the one and the red lights of the other flash alternately along the opposite shores.

Our boat, though it looked small and dirty at Constantinople, improved on closer acquaintance. The weather was beautifully warm, and the next morning as I came on deck, refreshed by a night's rest away from the pestilential air of Constantinople, I felt happy and cheerful. On the lower deck a curious sight met my eye. The steerage passengers had arranged themselves in squares lining the ship's side, and had warded off their separate sections with many-coloured cotton cloths, their mattresses were also gay with colour, and so were they themselves. Here on an Austrian steamer the lower deck had been converted into an Oriental bazaar. It was a marvellous sight. Some of the men were villainous to see; with fierce moustaches, horrible eyes, and swarthy faces, all armed to the teeth, they looked liked brigands out of a comic opera. Some had brought their women and children with them.

The food was coarse, bad, but plentiful, and the wines of Austria, which were served free with the meals, were pure and invigorating.

On our way to Trebizond, a journey which took us about three days, we made three stoppages at the three only Turkish ports of the Black Sea, besides Trebizond, namely Ineboli, Samsun, and Kiresun, all of them little better than villages. At each of these we stopped several hours, and got rid of some of our passengers. I made a practice of landing in the curious boats which looked exactly like the viking ships one sees in pictures, and are probably built very much on the same plan as the galleys of the ancients. The jabbering of the natives was like pandemonium. At Ineboli I saw a sentinel, sitting down in front of his sentry-box, his gun leaning up against it, and he himself busily engaged hunting for vermin about his person. It was a sickening sight.

Asia Minor is the land of promise flowing with milk and honey; flanked by Mount Ararat on the east, and Mount Lebanon on the west, it embraces a most fertile country. Rich in every natural resource, grain, wine, sheep, and other products, Asia Minor is nevertheless on the verge of bankruptcy, and this is due entirely to the iniquities of Turkish rule. The grain trade has fallen off, and to-day the principal exports from the languishing Turkish ports of the Black Sea are nuts and wood. Imagine an entire nation living on such a trade as that! The population is declining, and the land is rapidly becoming bare and desolate. As we sailed for miles and miles along the coast we saw few evidences of habitation. Here and there the lurid glare of the charcoal-burner's fire betrayed signs of life and human industry. The villages were wretched. The people live in houses built of matchwood with interstices through which one can look into them. They are erected on wooden piles, and under the first floor there are no walls. Here are kept the cattle, and what cattle! Bullocks, the size of an able-bodied dog, with their bones sticking out, looking more like pantomime monstrosities than real live animals. There is no butter in these regions, because the cows are so poorly fed that they do not produce any. The people themselves are wretched beyond description. Oh, the glamour of the East! It makes me melancholy to think of it. Whatever the condition of the Armenians may be, that of the Turkish peasantry is pitiable beyond description. One of the passengers on board our steamer was a young Greek merchant who was going back to his native place, which he had not seen since his childhood; he spoke a little Russian, and told me that trade was so bad in the Turkish ports of the Black Sea that most of the merchants were emigrating to Odessa or Batoum, where they had a chance of making a living, but that in Turkey something like a general stagnation prevailed.

The gendarme officer, who turned out to be a personal aide-de-camp of the Sultan, was the pink of politeness. All the English he knew was "Good-morning, gentlemen," but this he kept repeating whenever he met us. He neither undressed nor shaved all the time he was on board, but he did not look any dirtier than he did at Constantinople ; indeed, it would have been difficult. This gallant and intrepid officer supported life on some mysterious packages which he had brought with him, and smelt horribly of garlic and onions.

When we arrived at Trebizond we had our *tereskis* taken from us, and proceeded to the Hôtel d'Italie, the only hostelry at Trebizond. It resembled in many respects the well-known inn of comic opera. There was a large room in the centre into which the bedrooms opened out. Here one could imagine the celebrated Princess of Trebizond coming out at midnight and singing her earnest sentimental songs, much to the annoyance, no doubt, of the other guests, and meeting the chosen of her heart. The poor Greek who kept the hotel has since been murdered.

After taking our rooms we proceeded to the house of the English Consul, escorted by a cavasse. It was an interesting walk through the streets of this Oriental city, with ne'er a European in sight. In the market-place we saw crowds of camels with their Persian drivers in curious fur caps, and looking quite exceptionally dirty. They were mostly small, hardy-

looking men, and I heard afterwards that they were
not real Persians, but Persian Tartars, simple, honest-
looking fellows they were. Another curious sight
was to see an aged Turkish officer mounted on a
horse, and supported on each side by a soldier
walking beside him, over whose shoulder he had
thrown an arm. His toes were turned out like a
dancing master's, and his knees were also pointing in
opposite directions. He looked as though he was
a corpse which had been slung over the horse's back
and was being taken to be buried, but he was really
one of the commanding officers of the garrison.

As we crossed the spacious square of Trebizond,
which has a sort of garden in the middle of it, and
has some pretensions to beauty, we saw the young
merchants sitting in the dirty little cafés, drinking
coffee and gambling. In the narrow streets we had
continually to get out of the way of long caravans of
camels, whose monotonous bells reminded me of the
homely muffin man. Besides these Persian caravans
there were also Turkish donkey caravans, very
amusing to see. No carts are used. All merchandise is carried in packs on the backs of horses,
mules, or donkeys. Occasionally our cavasse unceremoniously shoved people on one side to make
room for us.

The town is built in a curious straggling way, and
we had to climb up numerous winding alleys, which
apparently led nowhere, until we reached the top of

the hill, where the residence of Mr. Longworth, the British Consul, is situated. As is befitting to his dignity, his house stands high above the town, and surveys the bay beneath. Yet in the case of Mr. Longworth, as in the case of most of the British Consuls whom I have since visited in the East, I noted a curious circumstance, namely, that he was entirely overshadowed by his Russian colleague. In Turkey and Persia I have indeed found that, as a rule, the Russian Consul generally took the lead, and was in all respects in a better position than his English colleague. He has better pay, spends more money, and keeps up a greater state. Whether this is desirable it is not for me to say, but it is nevertheless a fact that the Russian Government spends more money on its Oriental consulates than we do, and is very jealous of their prestige. Of course the Oriental mind is rather apt to judge of things and people by external glitter and surroundings, often mistaking appearances for realities, and hence the wisdom of the Russian Government can only be commended.

Mr. Longworth received us very pleasantly, and asked us who we were. We replied that we were English tourists who were on our way to Teheran, *via* Erzeroum.

"That is all very well," said Mr. Longworth, " but of course you are correspondents. It is much better to make a clean breast of it at once. Of course it is none of my business to cross-question you ; still, I must tell you that the Turkish authorities have definite instructions not to allow any Europeans to proceed into Armenia, and unfortunately for you, a gentleman has just managed to elude their vigilance, and has gone through. In these circumstances it is extremely difficult for me to assist you. Where are your passports ? "

We delivered up our passports with the docility of lambs.

" Have you taken out *teskerés ?* "

We explained that we had, but that they had been taken by the police on our landing. At this Mr. Longworth got very excited.

"Were they in order ? Where were they viséd for ? "

" They were viséd for Erzeroum."

"And do you mean to tell me that the Constanti- nople police viséd your *teskerés* for Erzeroum and let you go ? "

" Yes, we do."

"Well, that beats everything. You certainly have a strong case ; but you won't be allowed to proceed. You will be kept here for a few days, while they are telegraphing for instructions to Constantinople, and then you will be sent back."

This prophecy was literally fulfilled. We had to take up our quarters at the disgusting little hotel and wait for developments in the meantime. Mr. Long- worth was politeness itself, and sent his secretary with me to the Vali, or Governor, to intercede. This Oriental functionary was sitting in the courtyard of the Konak, or Government House, under a mulberry-tree, drinking coffee and smoking cigarettes. He was surrounded by numerous other officials, all sitting in a circle round him, and there was a continuous stream of persons soliciting favours, whom he received, listened to, and dismissed with a lazy good-nature really quite delightful to behold. He formed a curious picture in his red fez, grey overcoat, and cheap ten-and-sixpenny trousers. A man of comfortable rotundity, with a genial self-indulgent face, heavy black eyes, and a jet-black beard, he looked delightfully indifferent to all that was going on, and seemed to be laughing in his sleeve at the farce of Government in which he was playing so leading a part. He smiled upon me, showed a pair of bright red lips very full and heavy, and a magnificent row of regular carnivorous-looking teeth, listened to the Secretary, and then dismissed me.

Mr. Longworth did what he could to make our stay pleasant for us, and introduced us to the entire consular circle, which consisted of representatives of Russia, Austria, Hungary, Italy, and France. There was also a Persian Consul, but he did not receive because he had a Mahomedan wife. There were a few other notabilities in the place, and the order of life at Trebizond seemed to be very much as follows: Every day in the week one of the Consuls was at home, and received all the other Consuls with their wives. At these receptions cards were the only relaxation; but during the evening or afternoon, as the case might be, and at frequent intervals, servants in gorgeous Oriental costumes came in with trays, on which were various delicacies, which were regularly handed round. It seemed to me a very monotonous way of improving (?) the shining hours. The weather, however, was beautiful, much more pleasant than anything I had experienced on the Riviera, for there was an absence of that peculiarly malarial air at night, which makes the Riviera so dangerous. The people were all very charming; the Russian Consul in particular was delightful, and very pleased to meet an Englishman who had lived in Russia.

I was amused to find that when all these various Consuls came to return my visits, as in due; course they did, they each of them had much to tell me about the intrigues of the countries represented by the others. Scandal was of course an impossibility in a society limited to so few families, and political intrigue was a god-send.

The Russian Consul told me that although about two thousand Russian vessels put in at this port, nearly all the shipping at Trebizond was in the hands of smugglers, and that beyond smuggling there was very little trade. He also informed me that arms had been smuggled through Trebizond, and from Persia as well, in fairly large quantities, to the Armenian in-

D

surgents. Of these he spoke in very guarded terms, calling them unfortunate people. He evidently considered them the puppets of agitators.

Another Consul, not the English one, came to me and communicated the fact that the Kurds, whom the Turks had armed and uniformed, and given the generic name of Hamedji, were all in the pay of Russia.

"These Kurds," he said, "who are little better than brigands, have Russian gold pieces, imperials and half-imperials, which they pretend to have obtained in the ordinary course of trade ; but, as you know, the currency of Russia is paper money, and there is an agio on the gold which does not circulate, so that they could have got it only from the Russian Government. The idea of the Sultan was to turn these Kurds into a sort of Cossacks, to oppose the Cossacks of the Caucasus, but all that was only a pretext. The Hamedji would be useless against Cossacks ; they have been armed and equipped as a measure of precaution in the event of an Armenian rising."

This view, interesting in itself, throws some light on the general situation. There can be no doubt that the Sultan, at the time of the Sassun massacres, and for some years previously, was really in a state of considerable nervousness.

One evening, while I was sitting in my hotel chatting with my friend the artillery officer, and concocting plans, a visitor was announced. He was a mysterious person ; he insisted on seeing me alone, and would not give his name. I had him shown into my room. He was muffled up, but wore a fez. When he was alone with me, he threw back his overcoat, and revealed the most forbidding pock-marked face I ever saw. He had wicked, twinkling, little eyes, of which one squinted, and he was a miserable, weedy, little specimen of humanity. He could not speak above a whisper, because his throat was ulcerated. But on introducing himself to me, he produced a letter from somebody I knew, which convinced me that my friend at least trusted him. It would not be prudent for me to say more.

"What can I do for you ?" I asked.

"I am an Armenian merchant," he replied, "resident at Trebizond, and I can give you some valuable information. I do not want pay for it. I am myself a revolutionary, and I am anxious to tell you all I know. I have many sources of news. Turkey is an intolerable country to live in, and everywhere there are to-day revolutionary societies, ready to help to over-throw the present *régime*. The Greeks are quite as dissatisfied as the Armenians, so are the Turks them-selves. The tyranny of the police is intolerable. I know a case of a Greek merchant who has been transported because a revolutionary Armenian paper was sent to him to forward to some Armenian customer of his for whom he was in the habit of executing commissions. That unfortunate Greek has

been horribly tortured in order to make him reveal
the names of his confederates ; but the poor man has
no confederates, and knows nothing to reveal."

My informant spoke in broken French, which made
his communications still more ghastly. By the light
of a vile tallow candle, which was all the illumination
we had, and even that was carefully concealed from
the window, so that no shadow might betray him, he
looked indescribably weird.

" The state of Armenians is truly deplorable. In
former years we were wealthy and prosperous, and
Turkey flourished, we stimulated trade, the grain of
central Armenia was the best in the world. To-day
we are down-trodden and persecuted. In a court
of law an Armenian witness is not credited, and
a Mussulman's evidence cannot be shaken by any
number of Armenian contradictions, however circumstantial. The officials of the Government single out
the rich Armenians for their prey, conspire against
them, concoct evidence, and defraud and ruin them.
All commerce is at a stand-still, and it is not too
much to say that the whole of Asia Minor is ruined."

My informant substantiated these general statements with a mass of detailed illustrations, for which
there is no space in this short work.

" The Kurds," he continued, " are lazy brigands,
who go about in tribes and live upon the Armenians.
They are supposed to be shepherds, but they are really
robbers. The poor Armenian peasantry are very

industrious and good agriculturists, but all the results
of their labour are the prey either of greedy officials
or of these Kurdish robbers."

" Now tell me something about the massacres," I
said.

" All that has been published about the massacres
is true. The case of the poor peasants has been
under-stated, not exaggerated. But when you get
to Tiflis, which is a much better place for you to go
to than Erzeroum, you will get full particulars of what
has actually occurred; we here know little. But
there is one thing which I want to tell you. It is
supposed that these massacres were the result of
disturbances between Kurds and Armenians. That is
not true. Those disturbances were simply a pretext.
The massacres were deliberately planned and prepared by the Sultan at Yildiz Kiosk last May, and his
Secretary, who was the sole possessor of the Sultan's
notes, mysteriously died, and all his papers were
destroyed. Zekki Pasha, not the Master of Ordnance
at Constantinople, but the Sultan's brother-in-law,
and the Commander of the Army Corps, whose headquarters are at Erzignan, received instructions from
the Sultan's private Secretary to carry out these
massacres in every detail. The Sultan afterwards
disavowed Zekki Pasha's action, but he has presented
him with a golden sword of honour, and has generally
expressed his favour in unmistakable ways. I know
for an absolute fact that what I am saying is true, and

that it was the Sultan who planned the massacres himself. He personally hates the Armenians."

I have subsequently discovered, on my return to London, that the reason why the Sultan hates the Armenians is that he is suspected of being himself an Armenian, and not the son of his reputed father. I have also met lately in London an English civil engineer who was at Diarbekir many years ago when similar massacres occurred, and he told me that, through the telegraph clerk, who was in his pay, he ascertained that all the outrages perpetrated, even in their minutest particulars, had been dictated by the Sultan himself. How the Sultan controls everything, even to the smallest detail, the reader will have seen in the case of my visit to the Trop-hané. The Turk is, and all my informants agreed on this point, a rather stupid, but harmless and inoffensive person; it is the administration which is vindictive and cruel.

"In order to prevent exposure," my new-found friend continued, " and when the massacres were over, the authorities declared the district to be visited by cholera, and put a cordon round it, to prevent people going there until the snows covered up the evidences of their crime; but even now Europeans are not allowed to travel through the place, and you will be stopped and turned back, but when you get to Tiflis you will find out what is going on. All Armenia is in arms. All the young men are ready to shoulder muskets and march out to save their brethren, and the

Catholicos will place himself at their head. We shall soon be free."

It is a curious circumstance that at every place I went to I was always told that at the next place I should get better information.

"In Tiflis," said the Armenian, "you will find regular revolutionary committees ; everything is ready, we are waiting for the spring. Guns are being smuggled into the country, everybody is armed."

My new acquaintance, after consuming a certain number of bottles of beer, and an incredible quantity of cigarettes, in spite of his ulcerated throat, took his departure as mysteriously as he had come.

The next day I went to call on the American missionary who lived at Trebizond. He was a sombre-looking individual of true puritanical New England type, but he was not communicative. I was led to believe that the missionaries were making a small "corner" out of the news which they obtained, and were supplying, by underground means, the American press with sensational details, so that they regarded me as a trespasser on their preserves. They certainly do not live luxuriously, and seem to have to endure many hardships. The house in which the Trebizond missionary resided was very barely furnished, and did not even strike me as particularly clean. Beyond the following facts relating to the condition of the Armenian peasantry and their relations with the Kurds, I elicited very little information from him.

The Armenian peasants live in mud huts on the slopes of hills, and partially underground. They herd together with their cattle, which help to keep them warm at night, and their fuel is dung. Their principal article of food is a peculiar kind of dried and smoked meat. This meat they export, and it is said to be very unwholesome, and in some cases even poisonous. Their staple industry is wool and grain, besides cattle. The tithe is levied in kind, and there is very little money used amongst them ; but they are subjected to numerous and vexatious forms of taxation, of which I obtained more particulars in Tiflis. There are three classes of Kurds : the resident aristocracy, or beys, who are a sort of feudal lords ; the nomadic predatory brigands, who live by grazing, cattle lifting, and sheep stealing ; and the poorer subservient Kurdish peasants, who in many cases work for the Armenians and perform menial services for them. Still, the general economic condition of the Armenian peasantry is very bad, and they are in a chronic state of starvation and famine. The pressure of taxation is so great that the male population are in the habit of going to Constantinople, Batoum, and other towns in the winter in search of work. In Constantinople they are the water-carriers and dock-labourers of the place, and in the Caucasus they do the work of navvies, especially at Batoum, Poti, and other ports. The Kurds, I was given to understand, recognised no authority, and had to be coaxed and cajoled into allegiance by the Government ; they lead irregular and dissolute lives, while the morality of the Armenians, on the contrary, is said to be excellent, and their women, while very beautiful, are all that they should be.

Equipped with these scraps of information, and having heard that the authorities at Constantinople had definitely refused me permission to proceed, I took leave of my friend the British officer, who thought it would not be prudent for him to go on to Russia without special permission from the War Office, and prepared to leave Trebizond, which I must say is a beautifully-situated town, and in which I had spent a very pleasant week.

Before taking my departure, I had an illustration offered me of the peculiar state of the law in Turkey.

Mr. Longworth, when I came to say good-bye to him, was in a great state of excitement about a certain young Turkish nobleman whom he was trying to bring to justice, but without success. It appeared that this young man was openly defying the law. He was in the habit of going about with loaded revolvers, forcibly entering the dwellings of peaceable citizens, and outraging the women. He had wantonly shot several people, and had, at the instigation of Mr. Longworth, been brought up for trial ; but owing to the influence at high places of his mother, the proceedings had been quashed, and he was still at large, continuing his wild and lawless conduct. Mr.

Longworth had succeeded in getting the Vali to arrest him again, but he had once more been set at liberty. As far as I can remember, one of the servants of the American missionary had been subjected to his forcible attentions, and Mr. Longworth was justly indignant.

With this little incident in my mind I left Trebizond for Batoum, on board a Russian steamer, which was much more comfortable than the Austrian-Lloyd boat, and I carried with me a feeling that in the Turkish ports of the Black Sea Russian influence and prestige were the dominant features.

Another fact which I learned at Trebizond, and which I give with all reservation, is that the Sultan is supposed to be in league with his fraudulent officials, and is paid a commission on all bribes and pickings !

CHAPTER III.

THE transition from Trebizond to Batoum is a rapid change from barbarism to civilisation. It is a crude and rough form of civilisation, harsh and discordant if you will, but still it is civilisation. As soon as we entered the harbour of Batoum I could discover the stalwart forms of Russian soldiers and sailors, in their wide caps, keeping order amongst a crowd of Oriental riff-raff. These representatives of autocracy were dirty and slovenly, but in contrast with what I had left behind me, they seemed the pink of smartness. Upon their faces I could see no trace, as we got nearer, of that fierce and cruel fanaticism and that animal stupidity which cloud the countenances of the officials of the Sultan. I was in another world. Here was shipping of every description, locomotives standing on the quay with long trains of goods waggons waiting for merchandise, and a certain air of vastness and order, which is peculiar to Russia. The police officer who came on board to examine our passports was a courteous European gentleman, who

wore a look of calm dignity, which was very different
from the low cunning insolence of the Turks.

As I put my foot on land and looked up at the
glorious mountains of the Caucasus, I breathed more
freely. The very air seemed to be different. I felt
instinctively that I was in a great country, young,
energetic, and full of hope and promise. A little less
than twenty years ago Batoum was a small fishing
village, pestilent and vile. Its very name meant "the
end of everything," it was the *ultima thule* of Turkish
dominion in the Black Sea. To-day there is a
flourishing town, a town which has still many promises to redeem, but a town which has at least made
promises. Mr. Stead, in his book on America, likens
that country to Russia, and to me Batoum was
strongly reminiscent of a transatlantic port. Here
were the same low wooden houses, the same broad
streets, and the same air of work and of bustle. But
there the comparison ended. The people were totally
different. The tall wolfish Circassians, the poor ragged
Armenians, the broad placid Russians, these were not
features of an American city. Besides, there were no
cable-cars, no sky-scrapers, no newspaper boys, and
no bars. Of course it is the petroleum wells of Baku
which have given Batoum its impetus.

As I arrived on a Sunday I had to stay a day at
Batoum to get my passport inscribed by the police,
and so I put up at a very neat and comfortable hotel,
and then proceeded to take a walk.

I found the shores of the Black Sea lined with a beautiful and a handsome broad walk, not unlike the Promenade des Anglais at Nice, where the bureaucrats of Batoum, with their wives, sisters, and sweethearts disported themselves. The trip from Trebizond had been charming, the beautiful mountains of the Caucasus giving grandeur to the scenery ; but here at Batoum, where I had leisure to study them, the beauty of these mountains exceeded my liveliest expectations. In short, I was quite sorry to take leave of this quaint mixture of prosaic business and picturesque romance, but I was looking forward to Tiflis, the Queen of the Caucasus.

Here let me record a circumstance which I had omitted to note before. The captain of the Russian steamer which had brought me from Trebizond, and with whom I foregathered afterwards, was of Austrian extraction. The Russians are bad sailors. As I noted at Sofia, the Eastern trade of Austria is very much more important than is generally supposed. Austria is not the decadent country which some people think she is, and of late years her trade has made enormous strides. Whatever good qualities the Russians may possess, and they have many, among which their invariable good nature and kindliness are not the least, they have so far proved very bad traders.

The journey from Batoum to Tiflis was a revelation ! The road beats the Corinche hollow. Through mountain passes, amid deep ravines and steep precipices, now keeping the waters of the Black Sea in view, now along the valley of a romantic river, with steep and hilly banks, with the ruins of the castles of former robber princes frowning down upon us—the railway winds its picturesque course. True it is only a single line, and proceeds at so slow a rate that snailway would be a more fitting designation, but then that gave me time to admire the scenery, Here and there I came across tea plantations minded by the affable heathen Chinee, who had been imported with the tea by Russian tea-planters, who were anxious to make the experiment of growing tea nearer home than in China. So far I find the experiment has not been very successful, and in Odessa, and in fact all over the south of Russia, I found on my return that Ceylon tea was rapidly superseding the boasted caravan tea of which Russians are so proud, and which is generally not caravan tea at all, but shipped from China to London, and then sold to the large Russian tea-dealers. As the train slowly meandered on towards its destination, and I must say that the carriages were luxuriously comfortable, mounted Circassians occasionally came in sight, wearing their curious sheepskin caps, and equally curious capes. Horse and rider seemed to form part of the same organism. The men were all armed to the teeth, and were extremely handsome. Circassians have the air of princes, and indeed they nearly all bear that title. Their sharp regular features, tall elegant figures and graceful carriage, denote purity of race. They have a walk peculiarly their own which nobody could imitate. All the men are brave, and all the women beautiful. The women ride sideways, as they would in England, but wear the picturesque national costume; occasionally you will see them perched behind the saddle of their lord and master.

On board the train was an inquisitive Russian officer, who entered into conversation with me, and to whom I finally confided who I was. I am very glad that I did so, for he afterwards very kindly introduced me to some of the principal officers at Tiflis. At the time I had my misgivings about taking him into my confidence, but I thought it was better to make a friend of him than an enemy, and the result proved I was right.

He was a personal aide-de-camp of General Kurapatkin, the Commander-in-Chief of Russian Central Asia, and was just returning from a long journey in Europe, where he had attended the French and German manœuvres, and had also spent some time in England. He professed himself delighted with the British troops, and also spoke very highly of the French army. I ascertained that he was preparing an official report on the German and French manœuvres, but he was very reticent about the German army, though I rather fancy he had not formed so high an opinion of it as he had anticipated he would.

This officer kept pointing out to me interesting

features in the landscape, and at one of the stations he made me get out to see the pretty girls, for which this place was famous. He also informed me that the Russian Government had introduced silk-culture in the Caucasus, and had even established a model silk-farm, where the peasants could obtain cocoons and could get such technical instruction as they required. Subsequently, however, in Tiflis, I learned that this establishment had proved a ghastly failure, and that the Russian attempt to foster a silk industry had ended in a fiasco. The same, I also learned, might be said of the efforts of the Government to encourage cotton growing in the Caucasus. In fact, Russia cannot be said to have been fortunate with her State-fostered industries. Even the wine and petroleum trades are in a poor way.

Another occupant of the train was a drunken Armenian, who was making a debt-collecting tour. He was a genial blood-sucker, and told us, in intervals of hiccuping, that he was going to get out at the next station and intended to get his money there or die for it.

"If the scoundrels don't give me the money they owe I will sell up every stick they have in the place."

"Take care you don't get killed," said another fellow-traveller.

"Oh! I don't mind. They have threatened to kill me often enough, but nobody has done so yet. They dare not do it."

The man who had thus warned the Armenian turned out to be a railway official, and when the Armenian left us I got into conversation with him.

" What sort of a place is the Caucasus ? " I asked.

" Beastly place," he replied. " There is no law, no order, no anything. The people are unruly, and have been pampered and spoilt by the Government. They are all allowed to carry arms, and they use them. Human life is of no value, and the Government has no authority. It is a dreadful place. Did you see that fellow who got out ? That was an Armenian money-lender. He is pretty sure to get murdered somewhere before he has done. Those Armenians are the curse of the country. As it is they have got nearly all the land of the Caucasus into their clutches. The entire population is in their debt. They are sucking the life-blood of the country. The Circassians, are a lazy, proud, good-for-nothing lot of fellows who won't work, and care for nothing but enjoyment, and the Armenians have got the whip-hand of them. The country is going to the devil ! "

This statement quite took me aback, for in Russia I had heard the Caucasus held up as the most prosperous of the possessions of the Tsar, and the Circassian peasant praised for his industry and manly qualities. But things look so different at a distance to what they do at close quarters.

As it was very hot in the train, I went and stood on the platform at the end and admired the scenery we

E

were passing through. I had for my companion the
guard, a good-natured, simple-looking Russian, and
began chatting with him.

"What a pretty country!" I said.

"Yes," he replied, indifferently; "very pretty, but
all jungle. It is a most unwholesome place. We
Russians cannot stand it; it is malarious. There are
lots of Russian settlers here, but they all die of fever;
the climate is damp and unhealthy. You see, there is
so much rotting timber and underwood, which fills the
air with poisonous exhalations. We Russians lan-
guish in it. If the people were not so lazy, and would
clear away all this jungle growth when it rots, there
might be a chance for us."

Here was another illusion dispelled. The Caucasus,
the sanatorium of Russia, malarious! I could scarcely
trust my ears, and yet I had before me only too good
evidence of the truth of what the guard was saying.
We were going through a veritable jungle. Presently
the guard went away and I was joined by the inquisitive but omniscient Russian officer.

"So you are going to Armenia?" he said, incredu-
lously. "But how do you propose to proceed? I do
not see that you have a proper plan. You have no
base to start from."

"Well, no; I have no plan. I am going to try the
best I can. I thought of getting through across the
Russian frontier."

"That you will find very difficult. We are not

particularly fond of the Armenians. But, at any rate, I should very strongly advise you to apply to the Governor-General of the Caucasus for permission. If he grants it, you will have your journey very much facilitated, and if not you will be saved a great deal of trouble by learning the fact at Tiflis. It would be very unpleasant for you to be arrested at some little frontier town and escorted back by gendarmes."

I thought over this advice and felt that it was sound, especially as I knew the ways of the Russian police.

We arrived at Tiflis at midnight. For some reason, which it is very difficult to discover, the Russian railway engineers always construct their stations at some distance from the places after which they are named. Perhaps this is to encourage the local cab trade. Whatever the reason may be, Tiflis is no exception, and it took me quite half an hour to three-quarters to drive from the station to the town of Tiflis proper. Here I found an excellent hotel, the Hôtel de Londres, which I can honestly recommend to all travellers in the Caucasus.

The next morning I proceeded to call upon several of the Armenians who had been indicated to me, as well as on the editor of the *Mshak*, the great Armenian paper.

Before making these visits, however, I, according to my custom, took a turn round the town of Tiflis. Perhaps I was a little disappointed with it after all

I had heard; still, it is a pretty town, beautifully situated, and surrounded by glorious snow-capped mountains, and infinitely more civilised than vaunted Constantinople. It is very hilly, and some of the streets look like huge toboggan-slides; but the principal thoroughfare, in which are situated the chief public buildings, is really very handsome. Of enormous breadth, it is so wide that the houses in it are dwarfed by comparison with the vastness of the roadway. But the church and theatre, one in purest Byzantine style of architecture, and the other Arabesque and exceedingly quaint-looking; the palace of the Governor; the severely classical Museum; the somewhat tawdry Temple of Fame, wherein are preserved the trophies and mementoes of Russian valour in the Caucasus; all these, with numerous handsome shops and broad footways, on which are seen promenading officers in every variety of uniform —Circassians, Armenians, Turks, and Europeans— form a gorgeous picture. Speaking of the Temple of Fame, it is a curious circumstance that this interesting museum of war memorials is nearly always undergoing repairs, and for this reason rarely open to the public. If the European town of Tiflis is handsome and promises to develop into an extremely fine city, the Tartar or Oriental town is even more picturesque and interesting. This is the happy hunting-ground of the collector of Oriental antiquities, and while I was at Tiflis I found, staying at my hotel, a French gentleman with his wife, who spent the best part of his day revelling among the curios of the Oriental town, and picking up bargains, which he told me would excite the envy of his friends in Paris.

The Museum of the Caucasus is a model of what such a museum should be. The genial and learned Dr. Radde, its eminent curator, whose reputation is world-wide, and who is deservedly esteemed and respected in English scientific circles, took me over this building himself and explained to me his method of arrangement. He is a modern of the moderns, and has adopted the latest scientific ideas. Working on the same lines as Dr. Bowdler Sharpe in London, he has made his museum a veritable object-lesson. The walls are painted to represent the landscapes of the Caucasus, and his specimens of animals are re-presented amidst the surroundings and flora in which they occur. I was much astonished to find tigers and bisons included in the collection, and to learn that they had been shot in the Caucasus. The arrange-ment of the ethnographical section is also extremely instructive and popular. Weeks could be spent in that museum, and my only regret is that, as my book purports to treat of Armenia only, I must not dwell on this remarkable museum at greater length. I may, however, assure my readers that a visit to this interesting collection would alone repay a journey from London to Tiflis. It would be well worth the time and money to any intelligent person.

Should anybody be induced by this recommendation to make a trip to Tiflis, let me advise him to visit the celebrated sulphur baths, which are so luxurious and invigorating, and in connection with which the most remarkable legends exist.

As I have stated above, I called on the editor of the *Mshak* and found most of the members of the staff assembled. With the greatest courtesy these gentlemen placed themselves unreservedly at my disposal, and gave me access to all their information. I found that rumour had already announced my impending arrival, and that my visit to Trebizond in the company of a British officer was perfectly well known.

The editor, an extremely cultured and able gentleman, endorsed the advice of the officer whom I had met in the train, and strongly recommended my calling upon the Governor-General. He also informed me that Mr. Fitzgerald, the enterprising correspondent of the *Daily News*, was commonly reported to have been murdered by Kurdish robbers somewhere in Turkish Armenia. This was not altogether encouraging intelligence.

As I found there was a "consensus of opinion" in favour of my soliciting the permission of the Governor-General to travel through the Caucasus over into Turkey, I waited on His Excellency, who received me with that charming, graceful, and dignified amiability which is peculiar to the Russian courtier. But to my great surprise he informed me that he could not grant me the permission off-hand, but that I must await the reply that he would receive from St. Petersburg, whither he would be compelled to telegraph for instructions. "Our relations with Turkey," he said, "are in a very delicate state, and our Government is very anxious not to do anything that might be at all calculated to be disagreeable to the Sultan. In the meantime," he continued, with a wave of the hand, "you will remain our guest a little longer." There was a nobility, a graciousness, and an air of hospitality in his gesture which almost made me feel under an obligation to him, although I knew perfectly well that he was simply using a very ordinary Russian phrase, and that in remaining the guest of Tiflis I should find that my hotel-keeper would demonstrate his hospitality in the usual manner.

Owing to a break-down of the wires, I did not receive a reply from St. Petersburg for some weeks, and at the end of that time I was informed that I should not be allowed to proceed to Turkish Armenia. The intimation was brought me by a civilian official of the Governor-General's, who had formerly been in the diplomatic service, and had served, among other places, in Sofia and Japan. An extremely interesting man therefore.

"May I cross over to the Russian frontier?" I asked, "*viâ* Erivan and Julfa?"

"Certainly not," he replied; "the Government does not approve of your travelling in the Caucasus at all."

" Then would your Government have any objection to my going to Baku, and travelling across the Caspian ? "

The official smiled at my perseverance.

" You may go to Baku as much as you like. Baku is a commercial port, we cannot prevent you from going there."

" Thank you," I said, " I am very much obliged to you," and I was, for I wanted an excuse to visit Baku and cross the Caspian.

I next turned my steps to the Persian Consul-General, the famous Mirza Reeza Khan, who some time ago was commonly reported to have been engaged to be married to Miss Nikita, a well-known American prima-donna, who had given a series of concerts at Tiflis.

This wily Oriental diplomatist, who has since been promoted to St. Petersburg, received me with fitting dignity. He was magnificently installed in a sort of brummagem palace. I told him I was an English tourist, and that I wished to have my passport viséd for travelling in Persia.

Mirza Reeza Khan looked at me dubiously, and an incredulous smile lighted his countenance.

" I have had instructions not to allow any journalists to travel through Persia into Armenia. His Majesty the Shah of Persia is a friend and ally of His Majesty the Sultan of Turkey, and does not wish to do anything that might cause his friendly neighbour annoyance. You tell me that you are an English tourist, but permit me to inform you that even before you arrived I knew all about you, knew that I might expect you, that you were an English newspaper correspondent, and that you wished to proceed to Armenia."

I felt very flattered to find that my movements had been the subject of so much gossip, but I told His Excellency, Mirza Reeza Khan, that I could not be responsible for the rumours that might be spread abroad about me. Everybody was being suspected of being a correspondent. I had met an English officer at Trebizond, who was travelling for pleasure, and he was also suspected of the same crime. But I asked Mirza Reeza Khan to accept my assurance that I was in very truth an English tourist.

The Persian Consul-General again smiled, and told me that he was of course compelled to accept my assurance, and so my passport was viséd, and I paid a handsome fee. But I realised that my movements were being watched and giving His Majesty the Sultan some anxiety.

Presently I discovered another rumour that was being circulated about me, namely, that I was not a correspondent at all, but a British officer in disguise, come to spy out the nakedness of the land, and especially to report upon the state of the fortress of Kars, and the railway preparations that were in progress in Russia. Of course this suspicion arose largely from the fact that I had been travelling with an officer to Trebizond. On the whole I am not sorry that this was the case. It secured me most friendly treatment from the Russian officers at Tiflis, who used to lunch regularly at my hotel, and with all of whom I was on the best of terms. Some of these good-natured, jovial fellows spoke English perfectly, some had served on the Afghan Frontier Delimitation Commission ; they were all great admirers of everything English, were full of stories about the way the Cossacks and the English soldiers used to fraternise, and were generally most agreeable.

This fraternisation of English and Russian soldiers was indeed a very remarkable feature of the frontier delimitation, and considerably puzzled the Russian officers, who asked their men how they managed to understand the Englishmen.

"Oh! we get on all right, sir," the Russian soldiers replied. "We understand each other!"

"But what do you do? How do you get on?"

"We drink, sir, and they drink back. We understand each other. They are very good fellows, those English, sir!"

It was pleasant to learn that our Tommy had made so favourable an impression.

But one day all the officers came into the hotel looking most disgusted and angry. They complained of the beastly bore that they had to go through, of attending council meetings every day. Something

was going to be up next spring, movements of troops
were on the tapis, and all on account of those brutes
of Armenians. All those fellows were scoundrels.
One of the officers, who was stationed near the frontier,
complained that instead of being able to go shooting,
as he had intended, he would have to work all the
spring, and then he added :

"An order has been passed that no Armenian
refugees are to be allowed to cross the frontier, either
coming or returning. They are to be arrested and
sent back ; and if they won't stop when they are
called upon to do so, our Cossacks have orders to
shoot them. Pretty rough on the poor fellows. All
this is not their fault after all. But I expect the
Cossacks won't have the heart to shoot them. Ough,
that kind of work is disgusting, firing on non-
combatants !"

Thus the reader will see that, while I was waiting
for the Russian Government to make up its mind
whether I was to be allowed to go to Armenia or not,
I was collecting impressions. These desultory facts,
which I am thus relating in a rambling way, just as I
stumbled across them myself, when they come to be
focussed, as they presently will, if the reader have
patience, produce, I fancy, a very complete picture of
the general situation.

From the editor of the *Mshak* I got every assistance as to information for my journey across Persia ;
the editor of the *Ardzagank* was equally civil, and I

had not been many days in Tiflis before mysterious visitors came trooping in to see me, and to tell me what they knew and what they thought.

I learned that the *Daily Telegraph* correspondent had preceded me to Tiflis by about a week, and left for Kars; and one day I was told, by the editor of the *Mshak*, that he had obtained, from a trustworthy source, the intelligence that, escorted by a troop of Cossacks, the correspondent of the *Daily Telegraph* had safely crossed the Turkish frontier, and had arrived at Erzeroum. Seeing that my own progress had been stopped, this information edified me considerably; it made me begin to wonder whether the gentlemen of the Armenian press were at all familiar with American journalistic methods.

One thing, however, they told me which delighted me much, and that was, that seven refugees from the district of Sassun had just arrived at Tiflis, that they were the first batch of survivors to arrive, and that hitherto all information received had been from the lips of Moorish peasants, whose evidence was not so trustworthy. I was a little afraid that these Sassun peasants might have some affinity with the Cossacks who had accompanied the *Daily Telegraph* correspondent to Erzeroum; but, as will presently appear, there can be little doubt that these peasants were what they represented themselves to be.

Before, however, I give a detailed account of the interview I had with them, and the lengthy cross-examination to which I subjected them—it lasted three hours on one day and two-and-a-half another —I shall have to note down a few general considerations regarding the state of affairs at Tiflis, and the numerous currents, parties, interests, and intrigues in that very remarkable city.

CHAPTER IV.

THE STATE OF PARTIES IN RUSSIAN ARMENIA.

IN order to understand anything of the movement in
Turkish Armenia, it is necessary to know something
of the condition of the Armenians on Russian territory.   The real home of the Armenians lies at the
foot of Mount Ararat.   Here is the ancient monastery
of Etchmiadzin, here are populous Armenian villages,
which testify, by their prosperous condition, to the
industry and aptness for agricultural pursuits of the
Armenians.   To the north-east of Mount Ararat, on
the shores of the Caspian, lies the town of Baku,
which owes its prosperity and wealth largely to
Armenian enterprise.   If we cross from Baku by
steamer to Enzeli, and penetrate into Persia, we
shall find that the vanguard of Russian trade is
composed of Armenians.   When we enter the region
of the Caucasus from the Black Sea at Batoum, we
find again that the work of the Caucasus is done by
Armenians.   The dock-labourers, the navvies, all
those people who do the vague, undefined work

which the great industrial progress of the nineteenth century has created, are Armenians. It is estimated that in ordinary years about fifty thousand Armenians annually leave their native villages in Turkish Armenia to find work on the Caucasus. In Constantinople we have already seen that the hard work of the port is performed by the same industrious race. But Tiflis and Constantinople are the headquarters of the aristocracy and plutocracy of Armenia. In Constantinople, owing to unfavourable conditions, the wealthy Armenians prefer to efface themselves. They work secretly, and this habit of secret intrigue, peculiar to all oppressed nationalities, has here led to the development of those undesirable characteristics which have distinguished the Greeks and many other of the races subject to Moslem. In short, the Turkish Armenians distrust each other, they are not proof against bribes, and their political virtue is a doubtful quantity. Many of the spies and secret tools of the Turkish Government, whose name is legion, are Armenians. These Armenians have frequently misapplied the funds collected for national purposes, and can only be described as despicable people. Such Armenians will be found at Tiflis and Teheran, nay, within the precincts of the residence of the Catholicos himself. It is even whispered that the Sultan is of Armenian descent. This is one of the reasons why the present agitation in Armenia has not been more successful. The agents employed have not always

been honest, and the Armenian cause has often been
betrayed by Armenians.

If we glance at the map we shall see that Armenia
is a very large geographical expression. Although
Armenia proper has no sea-coast, the frontiers are
within easy access of the sea. Trebizond is practically
an Armenian port, which leads straight to Erzeroum,
the capital, and lived on Armenian trade, although it
technically belongs to Anatolia, a narrow belt of
territory, stretching along the southern shores of the
Black Sea. From Baiburt, the northern frontier town
of Turkish Armenia, which is at a distance of
about twelve hours' march from Trebizond, Armenia
stretches into Russia at Olti and Bayazid, and continues to the foot of the Caucasus Mountains and the
shores of the Caspian, including a large slice of Persia,
with the beautiful lake of Urumiyah. On the west,
Armenia practically begins at Alexandretta, and
reaches up north to Sivas and the port of Samsun.
So that it is not too much to say that to-day
Armenia really embraces the largest part of Asia
Minor and the Caucasus. The ancient empire of
Armenia was bounded on the north by Pontus,
between which and Colchis she inserted the small
end of a wedge, giving her a port on the Black Sea,
probably the Batoum of to-day, and by Iberia and
Albania. On the east her shores were washed by the
Mare Caspium, her southern frontiers were conter-
minous with Media and Assyria, and on the west she

was flanked by Cappadocia. Gibbon somewhat cir-
cumscribes Armenia in his map of the Eastern Roman
Empire, but even he, who is not particularly partial to
the Armenians, accords them a very handsome place
in Asia Minor.

Within the century the gradual awakening of
Oriental countries has not been without its influence
on the Armenians, and we find them constituting a
large part of the population of Constantinople, and
spreading themselves all over Turkey and Eastern
Russia, Persia, and even parts of India.

From time immemorial they have been a remarkable race, but their geographical position has made
their country the battlefield of empires. Alternately
conquered by Persians and Turks, they have thrown
themselves into the arms of Russia in the vain hope
of salvation. Gibbon says that their ancient Christian
kings or despots, " who arose and fell in the thirteenth
century on the confines of Cilicia, were the clients of
the Latins, and the vassals of the Turkish Sultan of
Iconium." The Cilicia of those days is the modern
Zeithun. He continues :—

" The helpless nation has seldom been permitted to enjoy
the tranquility of servitude. From the earliest period to
the present hour, Armenia has been the theatre of perpetual
war; the lands between Tauris and Erivan were dispeopled
by the cruel policy of the Sophies, and myriads of Christian
families were transplanted, to perish or to propagate in the
distant provinces of Persia. Under the rod of oppression,
the zeal of the Armenians is fervid and intrepid; they have

F

often preferred the crown of martyrdom to the white turban
of Mahomet; they devoutly hate the error and idolatry of
the Greeks; and their transient union with the Latins is
not less devoid of truth than the thousand bishops whom
their Patriarch offered at the feet of the Roman pontiffs.
The *Catholic* (Catholicos), or Patriarch of the Armenians,
resides in the monastery of Ekmiasin (Etchmiadzin), three
leagues from Erivan.   Forty-seven archbishops, each of
whom may claim the obedience of four or five suffragans,
are consecrated by his hand; but the far greater part are
only titular prelates, who dignify with their presence and
service the simplicity of his court.   As soon as they have
performed the liturgy, they cultivate the garden; and our
bishops will hear with surprise that the austerity of their
life increases in just proportion to the elevation of their
rank.   In the fourscore thousand towns or villages of his
spiritual empire the Patriarch receives a small and voluntary
tax from each person above the age of fifteen; but the
annual amount of six hundred thousand crowns is insufficient to supply the incessant demands of charity and
tribute.   Since the beginning of the last century (1600),
the Armenians have obtained a large and lucrative share
of the commerce of the East.   In their return from Europe
the caravan usually halts in the neighbourhood of Erivan;
the altars are enriched with the fruits of their patient industry, and the faith of Eutyches is preached in their
recent congregations of Barbary and Poland."

It is surprising to find how correctly Gibbon wrote
about this ancient nation more than a hundred years
ago.   When describing the religion of the Armenians,
he says :—

" Since the age of Constantine the Armenians had
signalised their attachment to the religion and empire of

the Christians. The disorders of their country and their ignorance of the Greek tongue prevented their clergy from assisting at the Synod of Chalcedon, and they floated eighty-four years in a state of indifference or suspense till their vacant faith was finally occupied by the missionaries of Julian of Halicarnassus, who in Egypt, their common exile, had been vanquished by the arguments or the influence of his rival Severus, the Monophysite Patriarch of Antioch. The Armenians alone are the pure disciples of Eutyches, an unfortunate parent who has been renounced by the greater part of his spiritual progeny. They alone persevere in the opinion that the manhood of Christ was created, or existed without creation, of a divine and incorruptible substance. Their adversaries reproach them with the adoration of a phantom ; and they retort the accusation by deriding or execrating the blasphemy of the Jacobites, who impute to the Godhead the vile infirmities of the flesh, even the natural effects of nutrition and digestion."

In a note Gibbon says that "it is from the year of Christ 552 that we date the era of the Armenians."

These short extracts will sufficiently explain the attitude of the Russian Church towards the Armenians. Upon that attitude much depends.

Having looked at the ancient history of Armenia thus cursorily through Gibbon's spectacles, let us now glance at the modern re-awakening of the Armenian nation. Here we shall find the influence of Russia all important.

Russia herself has only recently awakened from slavery. The close of the Crimean war and the death of Nicholas I. mark a new epoch in Russian history.

With the emancipation of the serfs, Russia has been brought face to face with new problems and ideals.

The emancipation of a population of over a hundred million people, all speaking the same language, obeying the will of the same master, appealed to the imagination of the educated classes of Russia, and led them to dream of the future great destiny of their country. Hitherto Russia had had little intellectual life ; she had been reclaimed from Orientalism by an eccentric and energetic ruler who had slavishly followed European models. Russian nationality was a thing to be ashamed of rather than to develop. Nevertheless, Peter I. was a Russian, and was followed by a line of Russian rulers. But Peter III. was a German ; his wife, who became the celebrated Empress Catherine, was a German, and her descendants, who have invariably married German princesses, can have small claim to be regarded as Russians.

These German rulers had little sympathy with Russian national characteristics. With the accession of Alexander II., and the emancipation of the serfs, there came a great change. Russia became a nation, developed institutions and ideals, and necessarily parties. At that time there were practically four parties in Russia. The Westerns, or European Liberals, the Conservative Reactionaries, the Anarchists or Nihilists, and the Russian Nationalists, of which there were two sections, the Panslavists, who were for expansion, and the Philoslavs, who were for the development of

Russian nationality from within. The Church party played a small and unimportant part. The alien emperors, although at the head of the Church, had little sympathy with dogma, and had inherited from their ancestress Catherine a certain weakness for French philosophy. Alexander II. was a German with a French education ; his political views were a strange mixture of doctrinaire liberalism and belief in the autocratic principle. In obedience to the liberal precepts he had imbibed by study, he was tolerant of racial differences and indifferent about religion. In his days the Baltic provinces and the Duchy of Finland were amongst his most loyal dependencies. The Caucasus under his brother Michael, who fully shared his views, was happily and beneficiently administered. Little sympathy was felt for that spirit of Russian nationalism which was then already gaining shape and strength. The Jews were tolerated, and enjoyed more influence and power than ever before ; the Armenians were the spoilt children of the Empire. Loris Melikoff was even made dictator of Russia.

But the outbreak of Nihilism brought about a revulsion of feeling, and the final murder of Alexander II. plunged Russia back into the Middle Ages. Everybody felt that things had gone too far, that liberal education and irreligion had undermined the classes, that freedom from control had debauched the masses. Something had to be done to save Russia from rotting away. In the meantime the Slavophil party had been slowly organising and gaining strength ; its secret societies covered the country. Its prophets, notably Aksakoff, had even dared to reproach the Emperor with want of patriotism, and had done so with impunity. The Heir Apparent had been won over to this party, and had placed himself at its head, and on his accession to the throne in 1881 the state of parties in Russia may be thus described :

The Panslavists and Conservatives had joined forces, but had been absorbed by the more vigorous constructive section of the Philoslav party, of which Katkoff was the leader. The Nihilists had been lost in the revolutionary or radical section of the Philoslav party, and the Westerns, the European Liberals, of whom Turgueniev was an eminent example, dared not lift their voices ; they were designated as unpatriotic, as renegades to their country. From henceforth, under the auspices of Katkoff, and with the aid of Pobedonostzev and the leadership of General Ignatieff, the reign of the Slavonic idea was to commence. That idea meant a sort of Tory democracy, or a national family, with the Emperor for father, the people for children, and the Greek Church for mother. Russian institutions were represented by the village commune, a primitive system of land tenure, and the artel, a co-operative labour association. The influences of Western Europe were disintegrating—they were to be kept out. The various dependencies of Russia, the alien races who owed her allegiance, were no longer to be regarded merely as appanages of the crown, they were the national heritage of Russia, they must be Russianised, and when once the entire Russian Empire had become homogeneously Slavonic, the regenerating influences of the Slavonic idea would be permitted to expand, until the whole world had been evangelised and saved from the yoke of Western materialism. It was a beautiful idea, and Alexander III. grasped it fairly well. He also understood that it was an excellent instrument of government, but he refused to allow its prophets to dominate him. Ignatieff's fall proclaimed to the world that the Emperor had so thoroughly mastered the Slavonic idea that he would allow nobody to interpose himself between the people and the autocrat. He also understood that unless the Greek Church was rehabilitated, he would be unable to retain his hold over the masses. Russia thus became, under Alexander III., a sort of fanatic religious empire.

The effect of this altered attitude towards dependent races and other religions was disastrous. The first warnings Europe received of the change of front were the outrages on the Jews under the auspices of General Ignatieff in Odessa and other southern towns. The Dissenters were the next victims. The Polish Catholics, the Lutherans of the Baltic, these have also felt the heavy hand of Pobedonostzev.

But perhaps the case of the Armenians is more pitiable still. Here is a nationality, possessing an ancient Christian faith, a beautiful language, and a rich literature, which have been maintained inviolate through centuries of oppression amidst hostile Mahomedan races. It is not likely that such a people should be wanting in tenacity. When the Russian armies appeared on the Caucasus, the Armenians welcomed their fellow-Christians as deliverers, and held out to them the hand of brotherhood. By their active aid Russia succeeded in gaining a firm footing in this part of the East. In the wars which Russia has waged for centuries against Turkey, she has always found helpful friends in the enemy's country among the Armenians.

She now embraces within her frontier a very large slice of Armenia. The seat of the Catholicos is part of Russian territory. Russian Cossacks patrol the foot of Mount Ararat. Erzeroum is within a day's march of the Russian frontier.

And the condition of the Armenians under Alexander II. was enviable. The Grand Duke Michael recognised their commercial qualities, the Emperor was grateful for their loyalty. They were allowed to follow their religion, to maintain their own parochial schools, to print their own newspapers in their own language. Owing to their superior education and industry, they became the dominant race on the Caucasus. To-day half Tiflis belongs to them. The great banks and commercial houses of that capital are Armenian.

But with the advent of Alexander III. and his fanatical creature, Pobedonostzev, the Armenians were made to feel that their religion, their language, their nationality, were threatened. Many of their schools were closed. When old churches had to be rebuilt, permission was refused. The Catholicos was snubbed, and a sort of general crusade was instituted against the Armenians.

The result of this has been to knit the members of this oppressed nationality more closely together, to make them feel that Russia is a cruel stepmother, and to inspire them with a sentiment of Armenian patriotism which had very nearly been extinguished by prosperity and ease. Where formerly the Armenians looked hopefully towards the gradual absorption of the whole of Asia Minor by Russia, they are now beginning to dread that consummation.

Indeed, the attitude of Russia towards Turkey has within recent years undergone a very remarkable change. When Turkey was a strong and formidable Empire, supported by powerful allies, Russia treated her as an enemy, and waged successive wars upon the Sultan until he had become so weakened that his former allies forsook him. Then Russia became the friend of the weak potentate. She will gradually draw him into the sphere of her influence until he becomes of about as much political importance as the Ameer of Bokhara, and practically subject to Russia ; then she will be able to swallow him whenever a convenient opportunity presents itself. Hence the Armenians, who were formerly useful to her, have become inconvenient. She does not wish to nourish any separate national tendencies within the confines of the Turkish Empire.

Thus we see that, both from the point of view of home and foreign politics, Russian interests are at present opposed to those of Armenia.

The Armenians fully understand this, but their attitude towards Russia varies.

One party, ostensibly the largest and most powerful, the party of the Mshakists, pretend still to regard Russia as the saviour of the Armenians, and consider it politic to maintain an appearance of loyalty and friendship towards their northern stepmother. Their arguments are as follows, and were expounded to me by their official leader.

In Turkey the Armenians are oppressed and massacred. Their economic condition is rendered precarious by the predatory Kurds, whose depredations are winked at by the authorities. What is left by the Kurds is swallowed up by the officials and the State. Their women are not safe. They are threatened with extermination; their condition is devoid of all hope.

In Russian Armenia there may not be as much freedom as the Armenians might wish. It is true that they are hampered in their commercial operations, in their schools and churches, that they have to pay the blood-tax by serving in the army of the Tzar, that their religion and language, their nationality, are threatened. But Russia is a civilised country. In Russia the lives of the Armenians are at least safe. They are permitted to amass fortunes, to teach, to follow the learned professions. They may enter the service of the State, they may hold commissions in the army, they may practise at the bar. Russia is a great country with large trade interests—there is room for everybody. If the Armenians are threatened with extinction as a race, it is better that they should be absorbed by a civilised state like Russia, than be exterminated by Turkey. Possibilities are open to them as Russian citizens which must for ever be denied them as subjects of the Sultan. They therefore pretend they would like to see Turkish Armenia annexed by Russia.

With this party the question of religion does not carry much weight. It is tainted with the liberal tendencies of a certain school of Russian thinkers not altogether inimical to Nihilism, and it secretly hopes that the present condition of Russia will not last. It looks forward to a great Slavonic republic, of which Armenia shall form part, a sort of confederation of Eastern European races, which will be allowed individual autonomy and scope to develop separate national characteristics. In Poland and on the Balkans we shall find similar dreamers. Stambuloff himself was once a believer in this view.

This party is composed of cultivated but weak-kneed people, who sympathise with the aspirations of Russian liberalism, who are as hostile to the Catholicos and their own religion as to that of Russia, and whose ideas of patriotism are merged in vague humanitarian internationalism. These are not the men of action. But amongst them are many agitators. They are the Girondists of the Armenian movement, and they will talk loudly of humanity, of freedom, and even make collections in aid of the cause; but they are devoid of courage, and are not made of the stuff of which martyrs are made. They would run with the hare and hunt with the hounds.

Then there is the religious party; the party which sees in the Catholicos the emblem of Armenian nationality, which cherishes a sentimental reverence for the literature and language of Armenia, and for all the national traditions, but does not go much beyond. Its attitude is more speculative than practical. To it belong a very large number of young men, of ladies, of Armenian nobles and merchants, and of course the priests, that is, those priests who have embraced religion as a vocation. There are, however, many political monks.

At the head of this party is the Catholicos, whose position is very difficult, but who, notwithstanding his great age, is a man of rare sagacity, eloquence, and energy. His attitude has so far been disappointingly correct. He has stirred up the hearts of his people to pity and sympathy for the terrible sufferings of their co-religionists in Turkey, but has not done much beyond that. He petitioned the Emperor for an interview, that he might intercede with him for the destitute Armenians, who are indeed sheep of his flock, but with whom he has little means of being in touch. The Emperor, however, refused to see the Catholicos, and though he has the legal right of audience of the Emperor, he wisely preferred not to put that technical right to the test. The Catholicos was elected for his vehement and patriotic eloquence, but since his election he has disappointed his supporters. He is accused of temporizing. But what is he to do? Some people thought he would put himself at the head of a revolutionary movement. He has the energy and personal courage necessary, and is still an excellent horseman. Of his fearlessness all will be convinced who have had the privilege of an interview with him. He is a noble and romantic figure, with a magnificent flowing beard, lambent eyes, and the mouth of an orator. His voice is magnetic. But he possesses more than the ordinary share of human shrewdness, and impressed me as a wise and crafty statesman.

Of his personal courage, it is related that, when attacked by brigands not many years ago, he shot one of them and got clear away.

Nobody reproaches him with cowardice, though he is accused of excess of caution. He must, however, know the difficulties he has to contend with, the untrustworthiness of the people who surround him, and the hopelessness of his cause. Perhaps he is wise in waiting for the intervention of foreign Powers, and perhaps he still believes that England will save. In any case he has by his prudence prevented an estrangement between himself and the authorities.

These are the two principal parties in Russian Armenia, but there are yet several more, which can be conveniently divided into two categories : the party of action and the party of quiescence or indifference.

The party of action is more powerful than people think. It has many sections. First amongst these, as being the most statesmanlike, is the national party, with the leaders of which I have spent many hours. These long for a free and independent Armenia. They do not care how it shall begin. If Turkish Armenia with Erzeroum should receive autonomy and be its nucleus they would be satisfied for a time. Nearly every able-bodied Armenian would emigrate from the Caucasus, and settle in this autonomous Armenia, whose frontiers would gradually extend, for no patriotic Armenian would be content with so small a national heritage. This party has already designated the future Prime Minister, and has a constitution carefully stowed away in a pigeon-hole. It is in touch with the Armenians of Constantinople, and also with the more active revolutionary Armenians. But it is at the mercy of spies and selfish intriguers, and is not at

present doing much, although it has the secret sym-
pathies of the vast majority of the Armenians.

The revolutionary party, which is secretly in touch
with the Mshakists and the national Ardzagank party,
have their ramifications all over the world. They
have organisations and secret societies in London and
New York, in Constantinople, in the Balkans and
Greece, in Persia, everywhere. They are intimately
associated with the remnants of the Nihilist party ;
they have friends even among the Kurds.

The Armenian troops of the Tzar are said to belong
to this party to a man, and nearly all the young men
of Armenia are its adherents. The vast armies of
commercial travellers which travel through Persia and
Turkish Armenia are all more or less members of this
party. Their agitators, educated at Geneva and other
European Universities, visit, disguised as peasants, the
villages of Sassun, Diarbekir, Sivas, and penetrate as
far as Zeithun. Many call themselves Americans, and
as medical men carry sedition, conspiracy, and rebellion
in their medicine chests among the rural population
of Turkish Armenia.

Van, Bitlis, and similar towns are full of them.
They are fearless, cunning, full of expedients, and
elusive. Amongst them are numerous spies of the
Turkish Government, and they can be little trusted.
They will be found in the service of foreign consulates.
In a word, they are ubiquitous. Some of them are
members of the ancient Armenian aristocracy. They

talk glibly of dynamite, and their probity is doubtful. They know all the mountain paths, and smuggle arms and ammunition, which they occasionally sell for their own profit.

I was assured that at a given signal all the time-expired Armenian soldiers of the Tzar would spring to arms, and that they would be joined by the bulk of the male population. This is a sanguine estimate, and necessarily conditioned by the amount of arms and ammunition at the disposal of the revolutionary committees. Still I think there is a good deal of truth in it, and the recent appearance of armed bodies of trained men apparently from nowhere, at Van and Zeithun, show that this statement was not a mere empty boast. When the revolt, which is now spreading all over Turkey, becomes more general, and Syria and the Lebanon, besides Macedonia and Arabia, have risen, we may expect the Armenians will be ready. I shall not be surprised if the present troubled state of Turkey gets more acute next year.

From this active revolutionary party, with its underground ramifications, its secret societies, its emissaries even within the precincts of Yildiz Kiosk, its American citizen agitators, who appeal to the United States' Minister at Constantinople for protection, let us turn to the purely passive party, their natural antithesis.

This is the party of vested interests and disappointed patriots, who, from self-interest or disillusionment, long for quiet. They do not want any revolutionary move-

ments, they have become indifferent to the fate of
Armenia. All they want is peace and security in
which to pursue their worldly avocations.

Among these we shall find many of the Armenian
officials of the Russian Government, the owners of
oil wells at Baku, the large class of usurers, and the
bankers, merchants, and capitalists. Many of these
have ever been selfish and occupied with the accumu-
lation of wealth, for which the Armenians have great
natural aptitude. But there are also very many who
distrust their compatriots. They have so often been
cheated, they have so frequently subscribed large
sums which have found their way to the pockets of
the agitators, that they have grown cautious.

While I was at Tiflis I heard loud complaints of
the indifference to the national cause of the wealthy
classes. But representatives of these wealthy classes,
whose hospitality I enjoyed, explained to me how
difficult it was for them to believe or trust in the
assurances of the various national agitators. I was
given an instance of the leader of one of the parties,
since deceased, at whose instigation a large sum of
money was collected for purposes of agitation. That
leader died, no record had been kept of the money he
had got together, for it was feared that the Russian
Government might confiscate it, and up to the present
day nobody knows what has become of this sum. On
another occasion a large sum of money was collected
for the purchase of, I think it was ten thousand, rifles,

if not more, with ammunition. These rifles were successfully smuggled into Persia. I saw the man who managed that part of the business, he is living in Tiflis now. But when these rifles arrived in Persia they were lost, all trace of them disappeared !

Too many repetitions of this kind of thing will cool the ardour of the most zealous patriot when it is he who provides the money. I have met men who have been ruined by too lavish gifts. There are, nevertheless, many wealthy Armenians remaining who contribute largely to the collections made on behalf of their Turkish compatriots.

Finally, there is the old school of Armenian soldier, the men who have fought side by side with Loris Melikoff and Lazareff, who are honoured and respected by Russians and Armenians alike, whose breasts are covered with decorations, and who do not understand the situation at all. These brave warriors burn with hatred against the Sultan, are full of loyalty for the Tzar, and do not realise that to-day the Tzar and the Sultan are to all practical intents and purposes allies. Some of these even write pamphlets describing the condition of the Turkish Armenians, and some subscribe towards their relief, but they are absolutely loyal soldiers of the Tzar, and are quite incapable of any logical political thought.

I have here endeavoured to give a sketchy picture of the state of public feeling among the Armenians of Tiflis. There are many contrary currents, many divergent streams. There are shopkeepers and bankers, journalists and lawyers, monks and priests, officials and soldiers, usurers and scoundrels, and amongst them all, moving about like vague undefinable spectres, are revolutionary agitators, mysterious individuals from America, emissaries from Constantinople, peasant refugees, and spies of all sorts.

But all these people are welded together by one common sympathy, by one great bond, the bond of language and brotherhood.

They are hated by the Russian population of Tiflis. And what is that Russian population? We shall look in vain for Russian pioneers of commerce, for Russian capitalists, shopkeepers, speculators, merchants. The officers are Russian, nearly all generals. The Cossacks and policemen are Russian, one or two of the schoolmasters are Russian, the officials of the Government are Russian, so are the railway employées, and that is all. England has to-day a greater vital hold over Egypt than Russia has over the Caucasus. Frenchmen, Germans, Belgians, one or two Englishmen, and Poles, Armenians, Circassians, and Tartars —these are the people who constitute the life of the Caucasus.

The few Russians who reside there loathe the prosperous and pushing Armenians who confront them at every step and elbow them out everywhere. The Armenian churches and priests are an insult to them ; the Armenian newspapers, the Armenian characters on the signboards of the smaller shops, the easy-going, comfortable familiarity of the Armenian and Circassian populations, their cordial relations —all these things are like gall and wormwood to the Russians.

Everywhere Russia has tried to impede the development of the commerce of the Caucasus. The railway from Batoum to Baku is only a single line. The oil producers of Baku have been refused a concession to lay a pipe. The mineral wealth of the Caucasus lies undeveloped, owing to Russian official red-tape. The port of Batoum, which was to have been free, has been closed, and so the trade between the Black Sea and Persia still goes by caravan, when time is no object. All goods going over Batoum have to pay the same duties as though they were destined for Russian consumption.

In the public schools of Tiflis only a certain percentage of the scholars may be Armenians.

To say that the population of the Caucasus are discontented would be to put it mildly. Both Circassians and Armenians are disaffected, and intelligent Russians are disgusted.

Such is the state of things in the Caucasus. Tiflis is languishing for want of trade, Baku is suffering from American competition at its very door, and the curse of militarism is crushing out the life of the people.

CHAPTER V.

THE SASSUN MASSACRES.

IN the last chapter I have drawn a sketchy and perhaps a somewhat blurred picture of the state of the Armenian population of Tiflis, and of those Armenians who, while sitting at their ease in comparative safety, are devising plans for the aggrandisement of their country and themselves. These patriots of the drawing-room and study rarely risk their own lives. The brunt of the indignation of the Sultan has been borne by the simple, honest, and courageous peasantry of Asia Minor. It is always the people who have to suffer. Of course it would be false to imagine that these honest peasants have not been prepared and led by heroic agitators, and that occasionally there have even been volunteers from Russian Armenia who have given up their comfortable homes for the dangers and adventures of a life of insurrection and rebellion. But they have so far been few, though I should not be surprised to hear that their numbers are increasing, and may eventually assume formidable proportions. Still, I

cannot help thinking that if the Russian Armenians
had been as prodigal of their lives as the Russian
volunteers in Servia and Bulgaria, things might be
very different to-day. I will give an instance in my
own experience. When I was at Tiflis and announced
my intention of making an attempt, at least, of
getting as far as Sassun, I was offered the services
of a well-known Armenian agitator, a powerful man,
who had travelled all over that district a year or two
before. Of course I gladly accepted his proffered
assistance ; but when it came to the push and I was
about to leave, I was informed that my guide was
prevented by private and family reasons from joining
me, and that it would moreover be inconvenient for
him to go, because if he once fell into the hands of
the Turks his life would not be worth a day's
purchase.

But let us turn from these highly-cultured gentlemen to the men who have faced the Turks in the
field—the Turkish-Armenian peasants.

I have already referred in Chapter III. to the
presence in Tiflis on my arrival of a number of
refugees, survivors of the Sassun massacres. These
peasants I succeeded in interviewing, once in the
board-room of the Armenian Benevolent Society,
and under the auspices of the Mshakist party, the
doctrinaire party, and once at my own hotel, when I
had for my interpreter a member of the Ardzagank
party, the nationalist party. I met them again by

accident at the house of a Russian veteran, who had
shown them a great deal of kindness. I can only say
that on each occasion these hardy mountaineers filled
me with admiration.

The three media through which I thus heard their
story were all hostile to each other. We have seen
that the Mshak and Ardzagank parties have totally
opposite aims, whereas the simple-minded old Armenian soldier was as unsophisticated as a child. Yet
on each of these three separate occasions the Armenian refugees told me substantially the same story.
On referring to my letters to the *Daily Graphic*, I find
the following passage referring to my interview with
these peasants :—

"On two separate occasions I submitted them, with the
aid of different interpreters belonging to opposing camps
of Armenian politics, to severe cross-examination. One
examination lasted three hours, the other two hours and
a half. There is absolutely no doubt in my mind that
these men told me the truth, for much of what they said
tends to upset the theory current here that there has been
no revolutionary movement in Armenia, and the cross-
examination to which I submitted them was so severe that
they must inevitably have contradicted themselves in more
than one instance if they had been telling lies."

It was not without difficulty, and only after many
futile attempts, that I succeeded in seeing these sons
of the soil. Having at last got them, I determined to
make the interview as full and complete as possible.
Seated at a long table with a green cloth on it, I was

supported by the Secretary of the Armenian Benevolent Society and several of its most influential
members. Three interpreters were present. One
had accompanied the peasants, one was supplied by
the Society, a third, a Turkish-Armenian gentleman,
who spoke no Russian, and consequently could not
understand the interpretations of the other two, but
who spoke French, had come at my invitation.

The Armenian peasants entered the room, and after
saluting me, and shaking hands in a charmingly frank
and simple manner, they sat down. They were very
sun-burnt, but had pleasant honest faces. None of
them exceeded the middle height, and they were all
young, able-bodied, active fellows, with curly black
hair cropped close to their heads, which were oval,
and strong beards of about three weeks' growth.
They had clear eyes, which did not shrink from a
close scrutiny. There was nothing fierce about them ;
on the contrary, they looked rather gentle and amiable,
and they were certainly free from those cringing and
fawning ways which seem to be inseparable from the
Oriental. Clad in an apology for European costume,
which they had got together hurriedly, they looked
very quaint.

I opened the ball by telling them it might be to
their advantage to inform me truthfully of all they
knew, because I was going to send an account of
what they would say to England. At this they all
seemed very pleased.

I then asked them whether they were Christians or Mahomedans. This question caused a sensation, and one of them darted looks of fire at me, and said something which I was told meant that he had not come to be insulted, and if this was the kind of thing they were to expect they had better go away. With great difficulty were they pacified. Two of them had been wounded, and had bullets in their bodies.

They told me they had come from Sassun, and were natives of the village of Galeguzan. It had taken them nearly a month to get to Tiflis.

"Now," I said, "tell me exactly what happened at Sassun."

They laughed, and replied that if they were to tell me all they had seen and all they had gone through they would have to talk for months.

"Well then," I said, "I will ask you questions which you must answer. What kind of peasants are you ; well off ? "

From their replies I gathered that they had been very well off indeed, and that their fathers had possessed flocks of sheep and cattle of all sorts. They had lived on good terms with the Turks, who were in the habit of collecting the taxes in the summer. The Kurds used to swoop down on them occasionally and lift their cattle, but on the whole they lived comfortably. It seems there were good and bad Kurds, and that some tribes were friendly.

"Are you afraid of the Kurds ? " I asked.

They showed their healthy white teeth and laughed contemptuously.

"No," they answered ; "we always thrash them."

"Now," I said ; "the massacres occurred last year, in 1894 ? "

"Yes," was the reply.

"Tell me what happened in 1893."

This took everybody by surprise. The interpreters in chorus told me that the massacres occurred in 1894.

"Yes," I said, "I know, but I want to hear what happened in the summer of 1893."

"In 1893," said the peasants, "the Kurds came and attacked us : there were two tribes, the Riantzi and Bagrantzi, and they attacked the neighbouring village of Talvorik."

"Were they beaten back ? "

"Yes, they were beaten back. We always beat them."

"Why did they attack you ? "

The peasants said something which seemed to annoy the interpreter, and the Secretary of the Society said it was of no importance ; but I insisted on knowing what they had said.

"Oh," said my Turkish friend, "the Kurds asked them to give up Murath, an agitator educated at Geneva, who had lived with them and was supposed to be stirring them up to rebellion, but they refused, and for that reason they were attacked." .

It appeared that the Kurds went to Moosh, the neighbouring garrison town, and reported the insubordination of the Armenians, complaining how they had been treated and repulsed, and exaggerating the armed strength of the peasantry. The peasants claimed to have killed thirty Kurds. The commander of the garrison of Moosh immediately sent troops to Sassun to punish the peasantry and quell the insurrection ; but the Armenians, on the approach of the Turkish soldiers, fled to the mountains with their women, children, and cattle ; and the soldiers, who seemed to be good-natured sort of people, finding the village deserted, returned without doing any damage.

Here I again put some questions.

" It seems you were armed. Where did you get your guns from ? "

" We make them ourselves."

Of course this answer did not convince me, but it was a great admission. It proved, notwithstanding what I had been repeatedly told by the Armenians of Tiflis, that the Turkish Armenian peasantry were armed, although they were distinctly forbidden by the Sultan from carrying arms of any kind, and it showed that the numerous attempts to smuggle rifles into Armenia had not all been as fruitless as I had supposed.

I now ascertained that when the Armenians were convinced of the departure of the Turkish troops

they came down from their mountains and returned
to their villages. One would have thought the incident was closed ; but it was clearly the cause of
the massacres. The refusal of the Armenian peasants
to give up Murath was probably reported to the
Sultan, who, in order to punish such insubordination,
planned the massacres which were to set his kingdom
in a blaze, and may cause the final dissolution of
Turkey.

The snows now descended, the winter set in, and
all was quiet. In the early spring of 1894, the
peasants said, the Kurds, mindful of the thrashing
they had received, showed no inclination to visit
Sassun ; but friendly Kurds informed the Armenians
that the Turks insisted on their coming, and collected
forty tribes to come and surround the district. These
tribes arrived separately ; altogether they were about
a month in coming. They came pouring in and
ominously camping round the district. The villagers
of Sassun, who had never before witnessed such a
gathering of the clans, suspected mischief, but maintained an expectant attitude. They had Murath for
their leader, who seems to have promised them help
from England. He apparently had two assistants, and
the village priests acted as his lieutenants. I strongly
suspect that my informants exaggerated the number
of the Kurds. It has been my experience that the
populace are rather inclined to over-estimate numbers.
But these tribes were not all hostile, and at least one,

the Harzan tribe, was friendly; their chief was subsequently arrested. I have heard it stated that these
friendly tribes actually took the part of the Armenians
in the proceedings which followed. Besides all these
wild nomadic Kurds, there was a battalion of five
hundred Turkish regular infantry, who were stationed
near the village of Shenik, and maintained a neutral
attitude. The Kurds were all armed with rifles.
The Turkish soldiers, who pretended to have arrived
for the collection of taxes, were supplied with food
and necessaries by the peasants.

It seems that the Harzan tribe had already warned
the villagers of Sassun of the intention of the Kurds,
and that the Armenians were prepared for what was
to follow.

"But," I asked, "how did hostilities commence?"

From the answer I received to this question it
appeared that on the night of the 19th of July the
Bragantzi tribe descended on the village of Semal
and tried to steal the cattle of the peasants. One of
the shepherds, probably a friendly Kurd, was killed.
The villagers immediately gave the alarm to the
neighbouring villages, and with combined forces
attacked the Bragantzi at daybreak, beating them
back with heavy losses and capturing all their cattle.
My informants now gave me rather a confused account,
from which I gathered that the Kurds reinforced,
made a fresh attack on the villagers, and were then
finally routed, losing large numbers. From this

narrative it seems pretty evident that the Armenians
must have been well led and were probably well
trained.   The Kurds, it would seem, had done all
they could to provoke the Armenians, so that they
might not be technically the aggressors; and had
not been attacked until they had tried to lift cattle.
The Turkish soldiers appear so far to have maintained an irreproachably correct attitude.   For a
whole month the Kurds and Armenians had been
looking at each other; in other words, the Kurds
had been blockading the district of Sassun.   It seems
quite clear that the plan of the Turks was to place
the Armenians in the wrong, and to leave the odium
of the dirty work to the Kurds.   In these calculations
they were destined to be mistaken.

The district of Sassun has in its midst a mountain,
the mountain of Andok.   After repelling the Kurdish
attack, the villagers of Sassun, with their wives and
children and all their portable goods and chattels,
fled to this mountain, where a sort of council of war
was held, and it was determined to resist to the
utmost any fresh attacks.   So, but indifferently
armed, as they maintained, they took up a strong
position on the mountain of Andok, prepared for the
worst.

The Kurds soon returned in much larger numbers
and attacked Andok, and now a regular siege commenced, which lasted ten days, after which the Kurds,
who had lost heavily, were once more compelled to

retire. It was at this point that Turkish intervention
and Turkish cruelty began. My informants were
particularly anxious to impress upon me that they
feared the Kurds but little, that they were always
able to repulse them, and that whatever might be
objected against these predatory tribes, they were at
least human beings, and perpetrated none of the
atrocities which have been laid at their door. These
the peasants insisted, and they were never tired of
emphasising the fact, were entirely the work of the
regular troops of the Sultan, hounded on by their
inhuman commanders. The Kurds actually refused
to have any share in the horrors which followed : for
these the Turks are alone responsible.

The Kurds retired before the Armenians, so at
least the peasants averred, and it is quite possible
that they somewhat exaggerated their own prowess ;
but the Armenians were not to be let off so easily
this time.

After the routing of the Kurds, Zekki Pasha appeared on the scene with an army of 70,000 of all
arms, including artillery. Here again some allowance
must be made for the curious difficulty peasants have
in estimating. numbers, to which I have already
alluded. I am assured that there are altogether no
more than forty-seven regiments of Hamedji in the
whole of Kurdistan, about 20,000 men, and that the
army corps of Erzignan, with all its subsidiary
garrisons, does not number more than 30,000 men at

a liberal calculation. Assuming that Zekki Pasha had denuded his district of troops and hurled all his forces at Sassun, that would have meant an army of 50,000 men. But although these figures are greatly exaggerated, there can be little doubt that a large army was collected and marched against Sassun. Zekki Pasha had had the whole winter to prepare in, and ample time to make his dispositions; and it is quite clear that the manœuvring of the Kurds was part of his plan, in order to prevent the Armenians from escaping, and to give him plenty of time to concentrate his troops. Zekki Pasha drew a cordon of troops round the Mount of Andok, and then proceeded to bombard it without any notice or warning. For twenty-five days, the peasants told me, did the bombardment of Andok with musketry and artillery last.

Owing to their knowledge of the country and the excellent dispositions made by their leaders, it would appear that the Armenians were at a great advantage, and that it was no easy matter to dislodge them as long as their ammunition lasted. But when this was expended they felt it was no use to continue their resistance, but decided on flight—flight by twos and threes. No organised retreat, but a sort of *sauve qui peut* into the mountains, where the Turks would have difficulty in pursuing them. For it seems that the Armenians had no illusions as to the clemency of the Turks, and a very shrewd notion of what they might expect if they should by any chance happen to fall into the hands of their enemies.

The Turks pursued them for forty days, and killed every Armenian, man, woman or child, whom they came across. Although the Kurds helped the soldiers in their chase, the peasants were very careful to explain that the Kurds themselves refused to slaughter the unfortunate fugitives. At last Zekki Pasha commanded a truce to the butchery, and the word was given that the Armenians were to return to their homes, and would not be molested any further. A proclamation was issued to that effect, and the wings of the wind carried the matter. However this may be, the peasants were evidently under the impression that such a proclamation had been issued, for they descended from their mountains and returned to their villages to find them burnt to the ground.

My informants arrived at Galeguzan in time to see their priest flayed alive and compelled to dance and sing, while soldiers stood over him with their bayonets ready to prod him if he stopped. He was singing the old Armenian hymns they loved when the peasants appeared. Subsequently he was thrown into the flames and burnt alive. On the site of the house of the Res, or village elder of Galeguzan, an enormous pit was dug, and into this were thrown the mutilated remains of one hundred men, women and children. This famous pit of Galeguzan was afterwards discovered by the European Commission.

Some of these unfortunate people were still living, and driven into the pit at the point of the bayonet, and then buried alive.

My informants were so terrified at what they saw that they took to flight again, carrying away with them the venerable priest, Petros, who they told me was a man of such wisdom and piety that people travelled great distances to see him, and that he was visited even by Englishmen! They were quite surprised that I had never heard of him, but the ignorance of journalists is proverbial! Hiding in caves they were able for a long time to elude the vigilance of the Turkish sleuth-hounds, but at last their want of caution betrayed them. Fancying themselves safe from pursuit they kindled a fire one day to roast some food at. The fire was discovered by some Turkish soldiers on the prowl who called on them to surrender. The peasants had only one musket among them and three rounds of ammunition. The principal witness, who was standing at the mouth of the cave and overlooking a precipice, was on the point of firing on the Turks, when the priest begged him to desist from shedding blood. It was an opportunity lost. Immediately one of the soldiers, who had laboriously climbed up, seized the gun and secured it. In an instant the peasant plunged his dagger into the soldier's breast and the two rolled down the precipice. When they reached the foot the soldier was dead and the peasant badly scratched, but otherwise unhurt. He looked up and saw one of the Turks slicing off his brother's ears, and another splitting open the priest's head with two blows planted crosswise over his skull. The peasants made good their escape, and I was told that the peasant whose ears were cut off was still living. The priest's body was cut up into small circular pieces.

Until November the refugees managed to hide in caves and forests, but they were at last caught and taken back to their village, which was destroyed. There was no shelter to be found, no food to eat. The peasants implored the soldiers, who had made an end of the massacres, to give them food or money. But they laughed at them, and told them to get help from their new masters, the English. The peasants now went to Moosh, and asked the governor of the town for food, saying that they were starving, and begged to be allowed to leave the country. For all reply they were marched back to other villages in the neighbourhood, and billeted on the population. But the peasants of these villages turned them out as soon as they could, for they were themselves in want of assistance, and had no food to spare for others. So the peasants returned to Moosh, and, going this time to the soldiers, implored them to kill them as they had killed the others. But the soldiers replied that this was not so, that they had killed nobody, and that the massacres had been committed by the Kurds. If any one should question them about the

events at Sassun they were to say that the Kurds
alone had perpetrated the cruelties. The peasants
told me that they had indeed noticed that many of
the Turkish soldiers had disguised themselves as
Kurds ; but they were quite certain that the real
perpetrators of the inhuman massacres had been the
Turkish soldiers. After this the soldiers conducted
the peasants back to Sassun. Here the priests made
a list of the missing. It was found that, roughly,
about 4000 of the original population had survived,
and that 12,850 were missing. I cannot think that
all these were killed, but so the peasants believe.
The peasants then erected a hut at Galeguzan, on
the spot where the dwelling of the elder had stood,
and where now one hundred bodies lay buried. Here
they left Avo, the nephew of Peto, the murdered
village elder, so that there might be somebody to
show the spot where the pit was. I understand that
the European Commission had this pit dug up, and
were disappointed to find so few bodies. Be this how
it may, my report appeared in the *Daily Graphic* of
February 12th, 1895, and the fact that the pit was
afterwards discovered is strong presumptive evidence
in favour of the depositions of my witnesses. Another
great point in their favour, and one which I wish had
been shared by the correspondents of several of our
leading newspapers, was, that although they gave me
a very circumstantial account of what occurred, they
did not harrow my feelings by dwelling upon re-

volting details. When it is once understood that the
Turkish soldiers were let loose to work their sweet
will, all further particulars are unnecessary. We all
know what that means.

Of course, a few horrible facts could not escape me.
For instance, I endeavoured to ascertain how they
were punished—for the peasants had told me that,
occasionally, when the Kurds complained to the
authorities of the behaviour of the Armenians, the
Turks would punish the Armenians. This conversation took place during my second interview with the
peasants at my hotel. They told me that sometimes
the punishment was death, sometimes the tongues of
the delinquents were pulled out by means of iron
tongs, which were occasionally made red hot. A
favourite form of punishment was to load the victim
with irons, provided with sharp projecting prongs and
rough jagged ends. The irons were then fastened on
so tightly that these sharp and rough ends entered the
soft parts of the flesh, and caused exquisite pain.
Another form of punishment was to brand the body
with red-hot iron. The peasants informed me that
they knew of a man, named Khloa Khazo, who was
then at the Moosh prison, who had been suspended
in mid-air by his feet, had then had his tongue pulled
out with red-hot tongs, after which a red-hot bar of
iron had been rolled over his body, and he had been
branded at intervals of about an inch apart.

I was unable to get them to tell me whether the

more ordinary forms of corporal punishment were ever inflicted. As to the treatment of women, the following instances, the least repulsive, will speak for themselves.

As a wedding-party was returning to its village, it met a band of Kurds. These at once attacked the men—I forget whether they contented themselves with tying them up, or whether they killed them—but they carried off the women into the mountains, outraged them, and then sent them back into their village. This is of common occurrence; the Kurds are continually waylaying Armenian women, kidnapping them, carrying them off, and then, when they have got tired of them, sending them back. I am told by Mr. Atkin, the Secretary of the Anglo-Armenian Association, that this practice continues to this day, and that the Armenian women of certain districts have petitioned Lord Salisbury for the help of England in this matter.

During the massacres a batch of ten girls was outraged by Turkish soldiers, who then offered to marry the girls if they would embrace Islamism. This they stoutly refused, and they were all cut into small pieces, with the usual Turkish repulsive cruelty, the details of which are too obscene for publication.

Many women, to escape from the Turks, committed suicide, previously killing their children; some of them throwing themselves from the tops of mountains into abysses, to be broken to pieces against the rocks.

One of my informants belonged to a family which had had ten male members ; now only five remained living. The others had suffered similar bereavements. One of the peasants had lost sight of his wife during his flight. They were a newly-married couple, and her loss had greatly afflicted him. But in a village in Russian Armenia he found her again. She had managed to get there before him, and one can imagine the joy of this unexpected meeting. Each had given up the other for lost.

I was told that the entire district of Sassun was desolate ; that there was not a habitation left standing except the hut over the pit at Galeguzan ; and, as the peasants vividly expressed it, that there was not even a sparrow to be found there.

I naturally asked the peasants what their object was in coming to Russia, and what they proposed to do ?

They told me that they had come to Russia for help—that is to say, to collect funds to purchase weapons with, and with the intention of returning to Sassun in the spring, in order to avenge themselves on the Turks. They told me that they had nothing left to live for, that they had lost their parents, their relations, their flocks, and that revenge was now the one animating passion of their lives. They told me that all the survivors of the Sassun massacres had the same sentiment. There was an old woman in the mountains who had had her hands and feet chopped

off, and was unable to walk, but could only crawl
along the ground; but even she was longing for
revenge.

"Vengeance!" they exclaimed, "vengeance is what
we want!"—and their fierce eyes gleamed as they
pronounced in deep gutturals a terrible "Akha!"
They explained to my interpreter that rivers of blood
had been shed at Sassun; that the blood had
streamed in torrents down the mountains; that they
had seen the things they had told me with their own
eyes—children mutilated, women foully outraged,
men killed and tortured, priests and people buried
alive. They said that I, who had not myself seen
these things, could form no idea, no conception of the
scenes they had witnessed. They said they knew
that death stared them in the face, and that they
must die either of starvation or at the hands of
Turks; but they wanted, at least, to kill a few of
the Turks before they themselves had to give up the
ghost.

I then asked them from whom they expected
assistance. And they replied that God above would
save them, and that they believed England would
also help.

I was much surprised at this answer, and am
inclined to think the Armenian agitators, who have
been preparing the peasantry of Turkish Armenia
for a national movement for the last few years, must
have spread this idea amongst them, otherwise it is

inconceivable how a number of ignorant peasants, living in a mountain district which, to say the least, is not easy of access, should have got general political ideas, and should even have heard of England at all.

The peasantry of Russia, for instance, think of England, as I know from personal experience, as a wicked witch living in a distant place, and plotting the ruin of Russia by means of cunning enchantments. England is scarcely a country to them—it is a person.

But the Armenian peasantry are evidently better informed. I felt constrained to disillusion these simple sons of Nature, and to tell them that there was little hope of England's helping them. In doing so, I must confess to a feeling of shame for my country, which has certainly not acted gloriously in this question, either before or since.

I then asked the peasants whether they did not expect any help from Russia.

This did not seem to produce an agreeable impression. The peasants looked indescribably disappointed and unhappy, and finally replied that they could see there was nothing left for them but to return to their mountains and die. Their object in returning in the spring was, as I ascertained, to build huts, and to save what little property remained.

" We must build nests," they said.

They also gave me to understand that they meditated concerted action against the Turks in the following summer, when the Turks would come for their taxes.

It is probably in anticipation of this meditated movement that the Russian authorities have given instructions to prevent the return of the Armenian refugees to their own country, lest trouble might ensue. I was assured by Russian officers that orders had been issued by the Governor of Kars prohibiting anybody from crossing the frontier, so that refugees from Armenia should not be admitted into the country, and returning refugees or Russian-Armenian Volunteers should not be allowed to enter Turkish territory. In this way the Russian Government has been rendering Turkey the same kind of service which Prussia rendered Russia in 1863, when she guarded the Prussian frontiers of Poland, and made it impossible for Polish refugees to escape.

I find that on February 12th, 1895, the *Daily Graphic* published a letter from me in which the following comment appeared: "If, therefore, something is not done soon by the Powers who took the Armenians under their protection, and then left them a prey to the Turk, the most fearful bloodshed may be expected." How prophetic those words were it is unnecessary for me to insist on. The massacres of 1895–96 have thrown those of 1894 completely into the shade.

While conversing with these Armenian refugees I mentioned incidentally that I had the intention of penetrating as far as Sassun if possible, and they instantly, and with great alacrity, offered to take me there themselves, carrying me over the mountains if I got tired. On the whole I am not sorry that I did not accept this friendly offer. I did not doubt the ability of these peasants to get me into Sassun, but whether they would be able to get me out of it was a very different matter. My duty was to try to arrive at some kind of an understanding of the Armenian question, and that could be better obtained by travelling about round the frontiers of Armenia than by penetrating into a country the language of which I did not understand, and with the customs and ways of whose inhabitants I was unfamiliar.

At a subsequent interview with these Armenian peasants I obtained from them a complete list of the seventy-four villages destroyed by the Turks, and this list is appended at the end of the present chapter.

All that they told me has been since confirmed in a very remarkable manner by the report of the Commission appointed to inquire into the massacres. In some details there is a slight difference. It was discovered, for instance, that the pit at Galeguzan did not contain quite as many bodies as had been expected, and the number of victims estimated by the commissioners is not quite the same. But we must not forget that immediately after the massacres were perpetrated the Turkish authorities proclaimed the district to be visited by cholera, placed a cordon of

troops round it, and prohibited travellers from visiting
it. Then came the snows of winter which covered up
the traces of their infamous deeds. We do not know
whether bodies were removed from the pit or not,
although it is highly probable that they were, and
that Avo recovered as many as he could find when
the snows had melted.

One curious confirmation of the story of these
refugees comes to me from Mr. Atkin, the Secretary
of the Anglo-Armenian Association, who told me
recently that the district of Sassun was all quiet,
and was in need of very little relief. This is not
surprising when we remember that of the 17,000
inhabitants only about 4000 survived, and that these
survivors fled. Of course some of the refugees found
their way back to Sassun, and erected huts and
dwellings ; how many we do not know, but probably
a very inconsiderable number. In considering the
story of the peasant refugees two circumstances force
themselves upon our attention. One is the fact, sad
and melancholy, that the revolutionary movement,
organised and fed by the more wealthy and educated
Armenians of Constantinople and Tiflis, was carried
out by the strong arms of hardy Armenian mountaineers, upon whose bodies fell the weight of the
Sultan's anger. It is sad to reflect that these fine
fellows have been killed, tortured and exterminated
for the political ambitions of others. As I beheld
these fine, honest, noble, and single-minded moun-

taineers I could not help feeling indignant at the selfishness of the ambitious wire-pullers who were hounding them to their destruction.

Another circumstance, equally forcible, is that these Armenian peasants do not appear to be by any means the despicable wretches which they have been represented. I think the cause of the Armenians has suffered by the fact that they have been painted to us too much as poor, helpless, miserable sheep, slaughtered by "a brutal and licentious soldiery." That view of the Armenians is not calculated to excite our respect for them, though it may arouse our pity. If the Armenians are really so helpless, shiftless, and invertebrate as people are in the habit of portraying them, then there would be small hope for them should they ever gain any degree of independence.

The popular idea of the Armenian is that he is a lazy, cunning, slippery person, who can be trusted to cheat anybody he meets, who has no manly qualities, and who can never be induced to do honest work.

I think I have already shown that the Armenian lower classes do not answer to that description, however accurate it may unfortunately be of certain types of small Armenian traders. The Armenians do the hard manual labour of the Caucasus and Turkey. They are not slothful as the Turks, and that they have grit in them their history proves and even Gibbon admits. We know that Lord Byron, who had no patience with grovellers, had the warmest admiration for the Armenian people, and the plain unvarnished story of these Armenian refugees does not exhibit them in a cringing light. It will interest my readers to know that they refused money from me, and only accepted a trifle after they had obtained my unwilling consent to their purchasing revolvers and cartridges with it. From all they told me it was abundantly clear that they were not afraid of the Kurds, that they fought like heroes, that they were armed, that they were industrious and had large flocks and all such goods as they required, and that they were not cowed, but intended to fight again.

These men, notwithstanding the terrors they have experienced, have shown themselves in every way worthy of comparison with the sturdy burghers of the Netherlands, who revolted against the persecutions of Philip II., and in some respects profit by such a comparison. They have no William of Orange, no wealthy nobles to lead them to victory, no adjoining sympathisers like the Huguenots of France and the German princes. Alone and unaided they have supported the shock of the armies of the Sultan, and well-nigh exhausted his resources.

These are heroes to be respected, not miserable wretches deserving only of compassion and pity.

Unfortunately the revolutionary agitators have not always been men of the same metal. Permeated by the vices inseparable from centuries of association with Turkey, they have come before Europe in the garb of miserable supplicants for mercy, astute Oriental mendicants. But if the agitators have often been wanting in manliness and courage, the same cannot be said of the peasantry.

The following is a list of the villages of Sassun destroyed by the Turks. I also obtained a map of the district, drawn up by a gentleman who had visited it some years ago, but this map, I regret to say, has been lost.

The Villages of Sassun destroyed by the Turks in 1894.

1. Galeguzan.
2. Shenik.
3. Semal.
4. Talvorik.
5. Hakmak.
6. Harthu.
7. Hart.
8. Purkh.
9. Dvalink.
10. Ekuter.
11. Isparank.
12. Hettink.
13. Arbik.
14. Dohal.
15. Ilantzik.
16. Mazere.
17. Sorik.
18. Bisharatkan.
19. Ishkhandzor.
20. Kalek.
21. Norhan.
22. Kissirkvarter.
23. Sevid.
24. Inguznak.
25. Sivok.
26. Pokhnatnin.
27. Navalay-Shavy.
28. Kovrasspi.
29. Mandedan-Kumani.
30. Murkoe-Damvin.
31. Balloc-Order.
32. Monnoe-Tun.
33. Mardastan-Ovid.
34. Ovaness-Damvin.
35. Akopuy-Tun.
36. Merguir.
37. Amakanin.
38. Tchai.
39. Gurdjok.
40. Kalekaneman.
41. Dapeh.
42. Dashtock.
43. Blur.
44. Kapre Sor.

45. Khissilgu-Arter.
46. Teretin.
47. Sevid.
48. Hatchkukh.
49. Tetek.
50. Orguin.
51. Kakhmatur.
52. Ardgung.
53. Karmir-Ard.
54. Khuissein-Tzik.
55. Herin.
56. Sardun.
57. Parka.
58. Ars.
59. Tap-Kar.

60. Bahamada.
61. Gremuri.
62. Akharon.
63. Kerervan.
64. Passur.
65. Ehu.
66. Idskar.
67. Shirged.
68. Konadzor.
69. Kaparnin.
70. Davala-Kajer.
71. Nertchi-Kalin.
72. Amk.
73. Khatan.
74. Kharipchari.

CHAPTER VI.

RESOURCES AND ECONOMIC CONDITION OF TURKISH ARMENIA.

FOR my facts in this chapter I am indebted largely to Colonel Lazareff, the brother of the celebrated General Lazareff, justly famous for his storming of Kars, an Armenian, and to the following works: a Russian translation from the Armenian by A. Arelyantz of Dr. Gregory Artzrun's public lecture on "The Economic Condition of the Turkish Armenians," delivered at Tiflis, and printed at Moscow in 1880; and another lecture by the same gentleman, translated into German by A. Amirkhanyantz entitled "Die Hungersnoth in Türkisch-Armenien" (The Famine in Turkish Armenia), printed at Tiflis, also in 1880.

After enumerating the principal towns of Turkish Armenia, Erzeroum, Hassan-Kaleh, Nariman, Alash-kert, Bayazid, Van, Bitlis, Moosh, Skhert, Diarbekir, Edesia, Kharbert, each of which is surrounded by about two or three hundred villages, three quarters of the population of which are described as Armenian, Dr. Artzrun says that Armenia is a tableland which has been called by an eminent German geographer, " Eine luftige Berginsel " (an airy mountain island). Of this Erzeroum occupies the most elevated part. The whole of Armenia is rich in minerals, for it abounds in mineral springs. At a distance of a few miles from Erzeroum, and in the neighbourhood of Hassan-Kaleh, there are abundant oil-wells, which could be worked very much like those at Baku. The natives employ the most patriarchal methods. They dip long poles with rags securely fastened round them into the wells, and when these poles have been sufficiently saturated with naphtha they use them for fuel and lighting purposes. Near Hassan-Kaleh there is a sulphur-mine, and there are also large coal-fields. At Erzeroum there are sulphur and iron springs, much prized for their medicinal properties. These springs seem to abound all over Armenia. Near Kagizman a kind of marble is obtained, which, when broken up, is so soft that it can be cut with a knife, but which, when exposed again to the action of the air, becomes hard. A kind of black amber occurs at Olta, the like of which is not to be found anywhere.

At Van naphtha abounds. Near Kamakh, in the province of Erzeroum, salt-mines and coal-fields occur ; but the richest salt district is near Moosh. It is estimated that Moosh is so rich in salt that it could supply the entire demand of Europe and Asia. Between Bitlis and Diarbekir a copper-mine has been recently discovered, but there are many iron and

copper-mines in Armenia. It is said that King
Solomon got his gold from Armenia, between
Erzeroum and Trebizond, and to-day we may still
find traces of ancient gold-mines in these regions.
There is a splendid silver-mine at Kumush-Khaneh
(the House of Silver), on the borders of the province
of Erzeroum, which is worked by the natives in the
most primitive manner. Lesser Armenia, or Cilicia
where Zeithun is situated, is quite as rich in minerals.
Here are iron and silver-mines, and the natives get
from the first the metal from which they make their
own weapons. Close to the town of Antapha there
is white and black marble.

The natural flora of Armenia is not luxuriant, and
the principal Armenian forest, near Erzeroum, now
belongs to Russia. The Turkish-Armenian population experience great difficulty in obtaining wood for
fuel and other purposes, and consequently dung is
used in the villages. In the towns the use of this
fuel is inadmissible, and consequently, owing to the
difficulty of getting fuel, many industries at Erzeroum
and other places have been ruined. Let us remember
that this was written in 1880. Of course it might be
urged that, in view of the abundance of coal and
petroleum, the lack of timber would hardly be an
insuperable obstacle to industrial undertakings. But
in order to develop the mineral resources of Armenia
large commercial operations would have to be conducted, industrial companies organised, and in the

I 2

present anarchic condition of Turkish misrule such enterprises would be impossible, owing to a lack of confidence in the Government and insufficient guarantees of security. This sentence describes the commercial prospects of Turkish Armenia as completely and truly as one could desire. For the same reason nothing has been done to artificially plant forests, or to import timber *viâ* Trebizond. In ancient days the Armenians were celebrated for their forestry and irrigation works, but of late the Turkish Armenians seem to have become wanting in energy and enterprise, and no wonder; besides, the communications are so bad that the importation of timber is next to impossible.

In some districts of Armenia the peasantry live in huts built of stone and earth, while the Kurds use a kind of reed or cane known as "stag's tail" with which they plait their habitations, which thus have the appearance of cages. The Kurds, being nomads, naturally prefer these lighter and less substantial erections, but wherever we go we shall find the Armenians attached to the soil and leading an agricultural life.

Turning now to the fauna of Armenia we shall find the country to abound in game. In the forests on the Russian frontier, and the jungles of the south, will be met every conceivable kind of wild beast, especially the stag, all kinds of mountain deer, buffaloes, bears, and even lions and tigers. I have myself seen a tiger nine feet long who had been shot in Russian Armenia, and it is not impossible that the small Persian lion may occasionally lose his way so far north as to penetrate into Armenia, but I confess to being a little sceptical about this.

From time immemorial the Armenians have been the horse-dealers of the East, and their pasturages are still famous, and may be said to be inexhaustible. During the Russo-Turkish war the province of Erzeroum was able to feed the cavalries of the Turkish and Russian armies, and yet there was plenty of hay and forage left for the domestic wants of the population.

Not content with the natural advantages of their immeasurable meadows, the Armenians labour to improve them by sowing all kinds of grasses, especially clover. It is probably for this reason that the Kurds have developed such a fondness for pasturing their herds and flocks on the succulent meadows of the Armenian villages, a practice in which cattle-lifting is only an incident.

The ingenuity of the Armenian peasants also exercises itself in improving the breeds of sheep and oxen. The size of their cows is remarkable, and they have sheep whose tails are so fat and heavy that they have to be supported on little two-wheeled go-carts attached to them. Armenian mutton is a great industry and is exported to all parts of the world. Dr. Artzrun says that the whole of Egypt is fed on

Armenian mutton, but he wrote in 1880: in those
days there were Armenians who sold as many as
20,000 and 30,000 head of sheep a year. The
Armenian peasant displays an affectionate gentleness
in his treatment of animals, indeed he shares with
them his home and his food. For instance, he is in
the habit of rubbing the hides of his bulls and
buffaloes with oil, so as to protect them from the cold
and give them a glossy appearance.

The Angora goats, who are so justly famed all over
the world, are not a monopoly of that region, and are
to be met with in the province of Van.

It is unnecessary to dwell upon the birds and fishes
which are to be found in Armenia. All those who
have travelled in the Caucasus and the East, and have
had the good fortune to taste the varieties of fish
which occur in the lakes and rivers of Armenia, know
what capital eating they are, especially when prepared
by an experienced Armenian cook.

We must now cast a rapid glance over the agricultural condition of the Armenian peasantry, and
here I may say that I am happy to be able, from
personal observation, to endorse the eulogistic comments of the learned doctor, who, being himself an
Armenian, speaks with pardonable pride of the intelligent industry of his countrymen. He says :—

"The agriculture of Armenia, notwithstanding the bad
government of the country, notwithstanding the fact that,
owing to its geographical position, it is completely cut off

from all enlightened countries, may be said to be in a comparatively flourishing condition, thanks to the fertility of the soil and the industry of the Armenian lower classes. It is (with a few small exceptions) nearly exclusively in the hands of Armenians."

The whole of Turkey is fed by Armenian corn, and if there were facilities for export Armenia could furnish forth no inconsiderable proportion of the corn that is placed on the markets of the world. Fruits also abound. Armenia is the country where the manna of the Scriptures is found. This manna appears in the early mornings of the spring and autumn on the leaves of trees, especially oak trees, in the shape of dewdrops. These dewdrops gradually congeal in the cold morning air, and are then gathered by the inhabitants ; they have a sweet flavour, and are exported throughout Asia Minor. They are supposed to be composed of the juice of the trees, which is exuded in the night air and adheres to the leaves.

The Armenians also grow their own wines, some of which are said to be superior to those of the Caucasus, and this in my opinion they might well be if they are ever to obtain the suffrages of Europe. One of these wines in particular is said to have a flavour which is half way between sherry and Madeira. If Noah's Ark really stopped at Mount Ararat, the vine-culture of the Armenians must have a very respectable antiquity.

Another industry of the Armenians is silk, in which also they do a large trade.

The population of Armenia is roughly divided into three races, the Armenians, the Kurds, and the Turks. The Kurds are mostly cattle-dealers, and roam about the mountains in search of pasturage for their herds and flocks, though a few follow handicrafts and trades. Thus they may be described as the gipsies of Asia Minor. Their wives assist them in their avocations ; they also make carpets and shawls. The Turks partly follow agriculture and partly trades or handicrafts. Their wives do nothing in the poorer as well as in the wealthier classes. The Turkish woman is exclusively her husband's plaything and the ornament of the harem. The Turks are clumsy workmen, and principally follow the trades of cobblers, saddlers, and other branches of the leather trades. Occasionally carpenters may be found amongst them. The Armenians purchase the rough wares of the Turks, ornament and improve them, and then sell them again. The higher walks of agriculture and the skilled trades are all in the hands of the Armenians, who are agriculturists, craftsmen, and everything. All dairy produce and cheese-making, for instance, are in the hands of Armenians. Particularly industrious are the Armenian women. Whether rich or poor, married or single, every Armenian woman, in addition to her agricultural work, follows some trade. The linen and cloth used in the house, and for the clothing of the family, is all prepared by the women, who also make linen, cloth, and silk materials for sale. All this is done by means of very primitive domestic appliances; the tools are made at home by the women themselves. Turkish towels, beautiful carpets, woollen stockings, shawls, silken goods, all those articles sold in the bazaars of Constantinople, are frequently the work of the industrious fingers of some Armenian woman; and so beautifully are they made that the European would have difficulty in believing that they could be produced by the primitive appliances used in Armenian villages. The Armenian women are besides distinguished for their beauty and modesty. A poor Armenian woman thus begins her work. She saves a small sum which will enable her to buy, we will say, a quantity of wool. This she will weave, and will exchange for a larger quantity of raw material. This she will again literally manufacture until she can exchange it for a greater quantity, and so on. She leads a laborious life, and it is said that an Armenian woman cannot keep idle for a single minute; she is always doing something. Even when summoned to attend a court of law, a frequent occurrence in recent times, she takes her work with her so as not to waste valuable moments. All the metal-workers in Armenia are Armenians, and all the artistic work is done by Armenians. They are excellent black- and locksmiths, and are celebrated for making a certain kind of secret lock

which is said to rival those of Chubb and Bramah.
They make their own rifles, copying the Martini-
Henry system, with which they became acquainted in
the Russo-Turkish war. The pictures in the local
churches are painted by self-educated artists, and
some possess considerable merit. Turkish authorities
bear witness to the abilities and application of these
remarkable people ; thus in 1862 a certain Khurshid-
Effendi compares, in a work on this region, the Turks
and Armenians, very much to the advantage of the
latter. He says the Turks are lazy, but gives the
Armenians credit for industry.

" Wherever Armenians live," says Dr. Artzrun, " their
agricultural and industrial ability, their public spirit and
their natural aptitude for culture, make themselves felt. But
this is more especially the case when Armenians live separately and free from the destroying influences of Kurds and
Turks."

In illustration of this the doctor draws an interesting picture of the villages which constitute the district
of Zeithun, the population of which has since, alas !
been decimated. He shows how these peasants
formed a sort of republic, governed by representative
institutions, and says that they were remarkably
prosperous and cultured.

Dr. Artzrun, having thus patriotically enumerated
the virtues of his compatriots, and pointed to their
many good qualities, concludes his paper with the
melancholy admission that these virtues are counter-

balanced by vices, one of the most dangerous of which is that strong tendency towards decentralisation and splitting up into small parties which I have had occasion to illustrate in a previous chapter. Personally I am inclined to think that too much importance may be attached to such so-called vices, which under favourable conditions become virtues, as in England for instance. On the other hand, we must not lose sight of the fact that the Armenians have been an oppressed nationality for centuries, that they have always been industrious and patient, and that they have broken out into revolt only when life had become impossible. In this respect they very strongly remind us of the Swiss people, who were philosophic enough to bear without a murmur the oppression of Austria up to a certain point, until their patience gave way, and the bands were snapped asunder after a long and heroic struggle.

But if we wish to understand more fully the present condition of the Armenian people, their hopelessness and despair, we must not neglect a factor which has been very instrumental in bringing about the present state of things—I mean the Armenian famine of 1879, which followed close upon the heels of the Russo-Turkish war.

For this purpose we will turn to Dr. Artzrun's interesting and admirable lecture on this subject, " Die Hungersnoth in Türkisch-Armenien."

He says that the famine embraced the whole of

Armenia, extending far into Asia Minor. From Erzeroum to Bagdad, from the Black Sea to the Persian Gulf, the entire stretch of country was destitute. He confirms these statements by extracts from official reports from different places, painting a most melancholy picture of the condition of the population.

What was the cause of the famine? The bad harvest of 1879 alone could hardly account for it. Previous to that year, the country had been devastated by a war, of the horrors of which we can have no conception. The fanaticism of the Turk was let loose ; entire towns, like Van, were burnt to the ground. The race hatred was something phenomenal. The Turkish Government had besides prepared for this war for two years previously. The taxes had been doubled ; men were taken from their work in the fields to execute public works for the Government, and so when the famine (the failure of the crops of 1879) came, it found a ruined population, already ground down to the last extremity, who had been compelled to expend their reserves and supplies, and were therefore entirely incapable of fighting against so great a visitation.

Nevertheless, as soon as the failure of the crops became known, the Turkish Government at once *prohibited* the importation of corn or other food-stuffs from across the Persian or Russian frontiers ! A reference to our own consular reports for that period will reveal a condition of things that would make any decent person burn with a desire to massacre every Turk he could come across. The officials of the Turkish Government sold the grain which was given them to distribute amongst the peasantry to usurers, who retailed it at enormous profits to the starving Armenians, or it was given to the Kurds, who also sold it in the same manner.

Space will not permit me to enumerate all the cruelties practised in that terrible year.

Dr. Artzrun points to all these contributing factors, and comments on the curiously infatuated policy of the Turkish Government, which is concerned in ruining its wealth-producing Armenian population in order to supplant them with lazy Mahomedans who have no aptitude either for agriculture or trade, and arrives at the conclusion that Turkey is following a carefully thought out political plan for the gradual extinction of all the Armenians in her dominions.

We can thus understand that the Armenian people, ground down by taxation and tyranny, decimated by the war, killed by the famine, have had barely fifteen years to recoup themselves in when they were overtaken once more by the vengeance of the Sultan, and to-day are nearer total extermination than ever.

There is therefore little cause for surprise that a nation like the Armenians, notwithstanding their many excellent qualities, should have been unable to show a stronger front to an overwhelming enemy, considering how they have been bled during the last twenty-five years.

Lest there should be sceptical people who doubt the oppression of the unspeakable Turk, and believe him to be so kind and amiable that he can never be roused to lift his little finger, except in kindness, against an Armenian, let us inquire into the incidence of taxation in Turkish Armenia and the economic condition of the people.

This is the picture which we shall find presented to us. The Armenian works, tills the soil, and produces; the Turk, his legal master, lives on him; the Kurd, his parasite, preys on him, and in the end, when he has given up all he has, he is massacred for refusing to give more, or for, at last, resenting the intrusion of robber bands, and driving them back with the arms he has himself manufactured.

To quote Dr. Artzrun :—

"The Kurd leads a migratory life, he is a nomad, his principal occupation is theft. Where the Kurd is found living side by side with the Armenian, he is his servant, he looks after his sheep, and attends to his horses. The Kurd pretends to be the true friend of the Armenian, goes to the Armenian church, talks Armenian, and offers up alms and oblations at the shrines of Armenian saints; he lives for years in the house of his master, and is his most trusted servant. But as soon as a favourable opportunity presents itself, he will leave the house of his master and run away to form a band of robbers, or to join one; he now appears as his master's enemy, robs and murders him, outrages his wife and daughters, plunders all his property, destroys his house, burns his fields and gardens. . . . As for the Turk, he is a listless, careless creature, accustomed to live on others. He can only command, but is incapable of work ; and he expects everybody to submit to his will. He believes himself to be created to rule, and others to obey and work for him. He regards all work as base and vile. The Turk lives at the expense of the Armenian. The Armenian pays the Government a poll-tax, fixed by law, but the Turkish official frequently arbitrarily exacts more than the legal sum. The Armenian peasant, besides the poll-tax, pays the Government one-tenth of all he produces.

"The collection of this tenth part of all the produce of the peasant is farmed by the Vali, or Governor, to a person (the publican of the Scriptures) who, of course, abuses the power entrusted to him, and collects very much more than his legal tenth share. This he can do with impunity, for the Vali himself aids and abets him. The Pasha, in letting a district to a tax-farmer, makes it a condition that he shall have a fat share of the pickings. Should an Armenian citizen embark in any trade, or on any undertaking, should he conclude a contract, or let or lease any business, premises, or land, you may be sure that the Pasha, the Kaimak, the Mudir, and the whole army of minor officials, including the Pasha's secretary, will all expect to get something out of him because he is ' making money.'

"The Armenian has no right to benefit by the profits of any work or undertaking without assigning a share of those profits to the Turk.

"Land in Turkey may be divided into a ' mioulk ' (private property), ' tafu ' (farmed or leasehold), ' vakf ' (church property, belonging to mosques and monasteries), and ' makhlul ' (land without an owner).

"Although the Armenian peasant is allowed to hold private property in land, this right, as we shall presently see, is frequently rendered nugatory by abuses. All land coming under the category of 'makhlul,' the Government arrogates to itself, and either sells or leases out on 'tafu,' handing the title-deeds over to the purchaser; nevertheless, the purchaser does not become the absolute proprietor, but has only a temporary enjoyment of the land. The Government remains the real owner. The 'vakf' is ecclesiastical property, but Christian monasteries and churches have no legal corporate existence. For this reason we frequently find among the official documents of the Armenian Patriarchate at Constantinople complaints to the effect that the estates of monasteries and churches have been declared 'makhlul,' and that the Government has sold or farmed out those estates without the least compensation.

"Pasturages are regarded in general as Government property. In proof of this we find that the Government lays a heavy tax on every sheep for the right of pasturing on Government pastures. . . .

"From the complaints of peasants to the Patriarch, it appears that when agricultural produce fetches a good price in the market, the tax-farmer who collects a tenth part takes the raw products, and, of course, a great deal more than his just share. When, however, the price of agricultural produce is low, the tax-farmer values the produce at his own valuation, which is then of course much higher than the market-price, and takes his tenth share in money."

Dr. Artzrun further states that in cases of the taxation of personal property in villages or towns where Armenians and Mahomedans live side by side, the incidence of taxation is always made to fall most heavily on the Armenians, while every preference and indulgence is shown the Mahomedans.

"The Armenian peasant," he continues, "either lives on

his own property or on Government leasehold land ; but the official protocols of the Armenian Patriarchate contain numerous complaints to the effect that the land of the Armenians frequently illegally finds its way into the possession of Turkish and Kurdish Beys. In this way the Armenian, who has never, throughout the whole course of his historical life as a nation, been in servile bondage, becomes the serf of the Derebeys.

"The Armenian who lives on the land of a Bey has to pay him a tax on his personal property, and a tenth part of his produce, in addition to similar taxes already levied by the Government. From the complaints it is evident that the land property of the Armenians is not protected from arbitrary abuse. Besides paying the Government the taxes enforced by statute, the Armenian has to bribe the Vali and his army of officials, etc.

"If an Armenian, by dint of his intelligence, inventiveness, and energy, competes with a prominent Turk, he is unceremoniously killed in the open day, as, for instance, Basturmandjan, a wealthy and important man, who enjoyed a great reputation and authority in the neighbourhood, and was murdered in the presence of the Erzeroum merchant, Khatchatur Effendi. Is it possible, in these circumstances, to expect any kind of progress in this country ? Is it possible to found any productive or profitable businesses, to establish joint stock companies, or similar associations?

"It is said that there are written laws in Turkey, but these laws remain a dead letter. An Armenian, being a Christian, has no right to carry weapons in Turkey, nor to give evidence in a court of law."

These considerations of the learned Doctor, founded on the protocols of the Armenian Patriarchate at Constantinople, confirm in a remarkable manner the evidence I myself collected at Trebizond.

K

Let us now proceed to examine what the actual legal taxes are under which the Turkish-Armenian peasant is weighed down.

Particulars of these I have obtained from Colonel Lazareff, to whom I have already referred, an Armenian officer who has made a life-long study of the condition of the Turkish-Armenian peasantry, and whose character and position give great weight to his statements.

This officer is preparing a pamphlet which will, he believes, throw considerable light on Turkish misrule.

In the *Daily Graphic* for March 18th, 1895, the following extracts from the list he submitted to me were printed :—

"The taxes of Turkish Armenia now in force have all been introduced since 1880, so that Turkish Armenia may truly be said to have a totally new fiscal system.

"These taxes may be roughly divided into four classes ;—

1. The Nufus.
2. The Amlat.
3. The Khamtchur.
4. The Intihal.

"The Nufus is a poll-tax, and is levied in place of the old tax for exemption from military service. In Turkey only Mahomedans are allowed to serve the country as soldiers, although, of course, in the higher grades of the army and navy, there are Christians.

"This tax is very grievous; every male, including children from the date of birth, must pay annually one Medjidje (or three shillings and sixpence), so that a father may have to pay five or six Medjidje a year poll-tax alone.

"Of the Amlats there are many kinds. The most grievous is the land-tax, which has been substituted for the old and easy Salian (which Sassun still pays).

"The Government has divided the land into three categories :—

      1. Alla, or fertile land ;

      2. Avsad, or second-class land ; and

      3. Adna, or sandy and rocky soil.

"By the old tax the peasant paid on an average five Medjidje a year, but to-day he may have to pay as much as fifteen and twenty Medjidje. The land is measured off arbitrarily by means of ropes.

"Then there is the Amlat for market-gardening produce ; this reaches £T.5 a year.

"Next comes the Amlat for hay, for eight cartloads of which the peasant has to pay a tax of two and a-half Medjidje. Formerly the Government took one cartload out of every eight for itself ; but to-day it has arbitrarily fixed the price at the above figure.

"Then there is the Amlat for brushwood, which amounts only to five grush ; but the Amlat for the right to make and use dung fuel amounts to half a Medjidje.

"We now come to the inhabited-house Amlat, which amounts to two Medjidje ; the cattle-shed Amlat, from one to three Medjidje ; the stable Amlat, also from one to three Medjidje ; the sheep-pen Amlat, from one to one and a-half Medjidje ; the straw-loft Amlat, one to one and a-half Medjidje.

"Besides these regular Amlats, there are the marriage-licence Amlat, which is only three-quarter Medjidje, and the emigration Amlat, which is also three-quarter Medjidje.

"The Khamtchur, or sheep-tax, is one-quarter Medjidje ;

and the Intihal, or succession duty, which includes the Kotchan, or tithe, is never less than £T.20, and often exceeds £T.30.

"When it is remembered that in an average Armenian hut there are often eight and even ten males, that a family has about three hundred sheep, and that the peasants emigrate annually to earn a little money during the winter, some idea may be formed of the weight of taxation with which they are burdened."

Nor should it be forgotten that these taxes are all in addition to the iniquitous tithe, or tenth part, which is so fruitful a source of oppression.

Colonel Lazareff informed me that the method of collecting these taxes was not mild. Troops usually accompany the tax-collectors, and these troops are quartered on the peasants, who have to lodge and feed them. In return for this the peasants receive stamped receipts indicating the quantity of food consumed, and these receipts are really vouchers, and, legally, the value of the amounts certified should be deducted from the amounts demanded in payment of the taxes. Usually, however, these technical details are but little respected.

Refractory tax-payers are brutally beaten over the head and shoulders with the butt-ends of muskets, and very often die under the punishment or from its effects.

On receiving the amount of the taxes the tax-collectors have to give a receipt, which is a certificate that the taxes have been duly paid. But very often the collectors refuse to give these official receipts unless they receive a gratuity for themselves.

Having thus enumerated the grievances from which the Armenians suffer, and formed some sort of idea of the burdens of taxation to which they are subjected by their ignorant and narrow-minded rulers, let us pause to consider their general economic condition. We have seen that the natural resources of Armenia are abundant; that coal, iron, copper, gold, silver, marble, and petroleum are plentiful; but that, owing to the anarchic state of the Government, these mineral resources remain undeveloped. The land is fertile and well cultivated. The Armenian peasant is an excellent agriculturist, his women are industrious, he is also a raiser of stock. Notwithstanding the heavy taxation by which he is ground down, and the arbitrary misrule from which he suffers, he is usually wealthy and independent.

But he has been visited by wars, famine, and butchery. The native population of Armenia is to-day decimated. His condition is therefore deplorable; nevertheless, he has to support two lazy races, the Turks and Kurds. His property is not safe, his women are at the mercy of predatory tribes, and his very life is in peril.

This is, indeed, a gloomy picture. Is it possible to imagine a worse state of things? Yet to-day that worse state of things has actually arrived. The greater part of the population of Armenia are starving and living upon the charitable contributions, but indifferently distributed, of foreign countries.

Can it be possible that such a state of things will endure ?   It is against all natural laws that it should.

Surely the limit of human endurance has been reached

CHAPTER VII.

SOCIAL AMENITIES.

LEST readers should conclude from what has been recounted in the preceding chapters that the Armenians are a soulless race of sordid money-seekers, out of whom all spirit and life have been crushed by centuries of tyranny, who are either sullenly thirsting for revenge and standing obstinately at bay, or, having forsaken all ideals and higher aspirations, are devoting themselves solely to the baser forms of commercial operations, I propose in this chapter to give my experiences of the social customs of the better classes of Armenians.

In the first place, then, let me say that the Armenian language has a rich and beautiful literature, a literature for the sake of which Lord Byron learnt it. This literature, which abounds in poetry and song, is not confined to such modes of expression, and has invaded the stage. At Constantinople there was an Armenian theatre ; there is one at Tiflis also. There are Armenian actors and actresses of great power and talent who draw largely, and whose names are

household words. In Tiflis Armenian plays are in
great favour, and are played to crowded houses. I
am told that these plays are instinct with humour
and pathos, and that in their interpretation Armenian
actresses develop a very high order of histrionic
talent. Needless to say that the personal beauty
of the actresses counts for a great deal.

The drama then is one of the amusements of
cultivated Armenians. There are also Armenian
writers of fiction, Armenian historians and political
economists; nor should the eloquence of the Armenian clergy be omitted from this enumeration of
the elements in Armenian society which " make for
culture." I have heard nothing to equal Armenian
orators outside Hungary. The eloquence of the
Hungarian orator is somewhat of the same order
as that of the Armenian: it is moving, impassioned,
but harmonious.

Armenian art is necessarily in a more languishing
condition, although Armenia has produced some
notable artists of the first magnitude, such as
Aivazofski, for instance, whose paintings were exhibited in London, but who is thoroughly Russianised.
While I was at Tiflis preparations were in progress
for an Armenian art exhibition—an annual affair,
I understand. I had not time to stay to see it,
but I was told that the collection would probably
scarcely repay a visit.

Nevertheless, Art and the Drama are represented

and find exponents. There is also Armenian music, there are Armenian concerts and Armenian singers, some of them famous, especially the women, who have beautiful voices—remarkable sopranos, rich and passionate contraltos. The music is not always joyous, melancholy strains and pathetic *motifs* seem to predominate, though these are not the only ones, and many are the wild lively airs that I have heard at the convivial meetings in hospitable Armenian houses ; contagious is their dance music.

We therefore see the Armenian race presents to us all the features of culture—a literature, a drama, art, music, and poetry. When in the next chapter I shall have to paint a picture of the life led by the merchants of Baku, a life which is not distinctive of any particular class or city of Russia, we shall have all the more occasion to wonder at the contrast, and be compelled to admit that even in Russia the Armenians constitute one of the cultured elements of the country.

The social life of the Armenians, as I witnessed it, is indeed very different from that of the Russian officers, functionaries, and merchants who live side by side with them. With the Armenians the family is the basis of life. You will rarely meet the Armenians away from their wives and families indulging in the orgies and dissipations of the restaurants and temples of vice for which Tiflis is as famous as Constantinople. Armenians rarely get drunk. I have never seen a drunken Armenian in the streets of Tiflis, although drunken Russians abound there. Yet the Armenians are a convivial race, they are fond of the pleasures of the table, and will, when establishing a "feast," spend an incredibly long time at the festive board ; but on these occasions they will sit side by side with their wives and families, and behave in a decorous and thoroughly civilised manner.

Young Armenians, who had been educated in Paris, and had tasted the delights of the wild life of the *Quartier Latin,* confidentially confessed to me their disenchantment on returning to their native land, where they found the conventional and moral codes much more stringent than in the gay capital of pleasure. As soon as a young Armenian arrives at the age of discretion he is expected to marry, and old bachelors are regarded with an unfavourable, not to say a suspicious eye. The young women are most carefully brought up and watched over. I never heard of, or saw, an Armenian woman of the unfortunate class. Constantinople is full of Greek and German women of doubtful character ; but there are no Armenians, so far as I could ascertain, in the ranks of this class of women either there or at Tiflis.

The young gallicised Armenians I referred to, complained that their difficulty was to find an Armenian girl in their own class of society whose intellectual training and general education was such as to make her a fit companion and helpmate. For this backwardness in the mental equipment of the average Armenian girl, the Russian Government is largely to blame. Only a certain percentage of the scholars of the high schools, both male and female, in the Caucasus, may be Armenians. As the educated classes of the Caucasus are principally of this race, and as this is the only race on the Caucasus which has any distinct tendency towards intellectual progress, this arbitrary provision is manifestly unfair.

For this reason the wealthier Armenians send their children to be educated either in Moscow or abroad; but of course this means a considerable expense, and consequently it is not possible for all.

Nevertheless, I have met in various parts during my travels gifted Armenian women of a very high grade of intelligence, devoting their lives with a rare and beautiful devotion to the education of the young, to charitable and public work, to the dissemination of " sweetness and light."

Another difficulty in the way of the higher education of Armenian women is caused by the custom of contracting early marriages. This is the curse of the East. We have all heard of the child marriages of India; in Persia it is usual for a girl to be married at the age of eleven, and hence it is not surprising to find girls of fourteen among the married women of Armenia.

Seeing that convivial gatherings play an important part in the amusements of the Armenians, and that the amusements of a people are an index to their character, I will now relate my own experience of Armenian dinner-parties.

The first and largest I ever attended was given by an Armenian widow lady, much respected for her many charities, and the mother of a large and prosperous family. The members of this family, with its numerous collateral adherents, were all invited to meet me. It was a big feast. The time appointed was half-past three, and I arrived to the minute. I found the spacious room of my hostess's apartment filled with people: many charming young ladies, several officers, a Georgian prince, and a number of civilians. What was my surprise to discover them all drinking coffee and smoking cigarettes! Could it be that I had mistaken the hour of dinner and arrived after the feast! Presently my doubts were set at rest and dinner was announced. We sat down in a large saloon, along three walls of which tables were ranged. The ladies all sat side by side, the men facing them. Vodka and zakouska, or *hors d'œuvres*, were now produced, and then a sumptuous banquet was served, at which we remained seated from half-past four to eight. It was excellently cooked, but the fish came last, rather an inversion of the European order. Before we commenced dinner a toastmaster was elected, and he appointed an assistant. I was told that this was an invariable custom at all Armenian dinners, and that the gentleman elected

was a man of great experience in these matters. I
was soon to see what his functions were. We had
scarcely begun dinner before the toastmaster rose and
carefully inspected the table, his eagle eye passing
our glasses in rapid review. Then he ordered us to
charge our glasses, and informed us that he meant
business, and would not allow any scamping of the
important duties which awaited us. The first toast
proposed was that of the Emperor. We had to drink
this standing and drain our glasses. The toastmaster
and his assistant afterwards ascertained that we had
complied with this necessary formality. Then we sat
down, and we had music. One man whacked an
enormous tambourine, while another played a curious
kind of lute, a cross between a guitar, a mandoline,
and a banjo. We then drank the health of the
Queen of England in the same manner, which was
followed by the same honours. Then we drank to
the British Press, and we drank confusion to Turkey,
and the health of every individual in the room, and
all their cousins, always standing. Towards the end
of dinner the fun grew fast and furious. After the
toasts, ladies got up and danced the national Lisguinka ; and even when dinner was over we remained
seated for a long time, like the famous monks, re-
membering one saint more. It was an extremely
jovial meeting, and impressed me very favourably.

I have dined and supped at numerous other
Armenian houses, but always found a very similar

order of ceremony adhered to, and always the same whole-hearted joviality. The Armenians are all fond of speechifying, and make very good, very amusing, and sometimes very eloquent and pathetic speeches. At one dinner to which I was invited, national and ancient Armenian songs were sung with great artistic effect.

At a supper, given by a wealthy Armenian merchant, to which I was bidden, a different state of things obtained. The surroundings were such as might have been found in any wealthy house in Paris or Berlin. The apartments of my host were most interesting. The walls were hung with rare etchings and pictures, his bookshelves contained a most perfect library of rare books, among them a complete collection of ancient and modern Armenian literature, many of the specimens in quaint and beautiful bindings. The conversation was most cultured, the guests had the most distinguished manners and that perfect ease and grace which are characteristic of good breeding. Here of course there were no toastmasters and no quaint national customs.

But on another occasion I had an opportunity of witnessing an Armenian wedding, and that was very curious. It was celebrated in the evening. The family belonged to the wealthy merchant class, and occupied a very handsome flat in the principal street of Tiflis, where the Governor-General's palace and nearly all the public buildings are situated. The

bride and bridesmaids were in white, and the bride
had a beautiful veil which fell to her feet, and the
usual wreath of orange blossoms. The men were
dressed in the conventional evening dress of the
nineteenth century, but there were many officers
present in uniform, and a goodly number of well-
decorated generals, without whom no party in the
dominions of the Tzar can make any pretensions to
fashion.

The grand main staircase was covered with a handsome red carpet, and profusely decorated with palms,
laurels, and evergreens. After the ceremony in
church, whither the party proceeded in numerous
carriages, after previously assembling in the apartment
of the bride's father, the return of the bride and
bridegroom was announced by Bengal lights. Two
priests in their sacerdotal robes of cloth of gold
ascended the stairs and took up a position on a
landing, holding massive candles in handsome candle-
sticks, which were now lighted. These priests in
their curious hats, resembling that of a Jewish Rabbi,
with flowing beards and hair hanging down to their
shoulders, looked solemn, venerable, and imposing.
Soon there were more Bengal lights, and the bridal
procession formed at the foot of the stairs and
ascended them, the bride and bridegroom leading the
way. The priests now began a solemn chant as the
bride and bridegroom, now husband and wife, approached ; flanking the priests stood two gentlemen

in evening dress, each with a drawn sword in his
hand. As the newly-married couple arrived at the
landing where the priests were waiting to receive
them, these two gentlemen crossed their swords in
mid-air, thus forming an arch under which the
husband and wife stood while the priests blessed and
kissed them.

The priests, bearing the candles alight, now preceded the bridal procession into the apartment, where
a hospitable supper was spread, which was followed by
rollicking fun, the dancing of the Lisguinka, singing
and revelry, which was continued long into the night,
and after the wedded pair had departed for their
honeymoon.

On another occasion I had an opportunity of seeing
the youth and beauty of Armenian fashion : a grand
ball was given at the Nobles' Club of Tiflis by the
Armenian community. These balls are of frequent
occurrence at Tiflis during the winter, but this
particular one had been got up for the benefit of the
sufferers from the massacres, and it was a point of
honour for all Armenians of any pretensions to social
position, to attend. The committee did me the
honour of inviting me, and of course I went. I may
say that I was fairly astonished with what I saw.
The handsome saloons of the Nobles' Club were
crammed ; I believe there were something like five
hundred people present. Never, not even in Paris,
have I seen a more brilliant gathering, more elegant

toilettes, more taste, beauty, and *chic*. Several great ladies and Armenian princesses had arrived from Constantinople on purpose to give the ball the lustre of their presence. Many of these had flower stalls, where bouquets and buttonholes, principally roses, were sold. It is a common belief that all Armenian women are dark, languorous, and Oriental-looking ; but this idea is erroneous, there is a fair type of Armenian as well as a dark, and I can only say that the great ladies, young, beautiful, and graceful, whom I saw collected at this ball, were fairly dazzling. These Armenian ladies spoke French, German, and Russian, some of them even English. They were surrounded by distinguished-looking men, and it was a revelation to see the number of Armenian officers wearing the Russian uniform.

The ball was a brilliant success, it was conducted on European lines and might have taken place at Paris, Berlin, or Vienna, or even St. Petersburg ; and to judge by the surroundings and demeanour of everybody, one would scarcely have believed that it was going on in a provincial town like Tiflis, inhabited principally by pensioned Georgian generals.

Enough has been said to show that the Armenians are far from being an uncultured, uncivilised people. But those who think that refined pleasures, polite literature, artistic tastes, and elegant genial social habits are not sufficient to establish a claim for the consideration of cultured Europe, had better turn to

L

the records of the universities of Paris, Geneva, Berlin, and other university towns, and hear in what estimation the Armenian students are held there. Armenian professors lecturing on scientific branches of study will be found scattered over the entire globe. The Russian minister of education, Delyanoff, is an Armenian.

It may be objected against the Armenians as a race that they have no national athletic games, and cannot, therefore, find in their national life that stimulus for activity which has given England her supremacy, and which founded the Olympian games of Greece. How can we expect a nation ground down by taxes to play when they have had to spend their lives in work? Besides, the Armenians are not singular in this respect. The Turks and Persians, the Russians, and in fact all the neighbouring races, are more distinguished for their indolence than their fondness of games.

But then the Armenians, in common with nearly all Orientals, are gamblers—that unfortunately cannot be denied. It is a vice, however, which they share with the majority of the inhabitants of the globe.

CHAPTER VIII.

BAKU.

HAVING been prohibited by the Russian Government from crossing over the Russian frontier either into Turkish or Persian territory, it was necessary for me to try to get to Persia across the Caspian, and thence ride back. Baku is a commercial town, and there is considerable commercial intercourse between Persia and Russia, so that the Government informed me that they could not object to my taking this route.

I had collected sufficient materials in Tiflis and was anxious to push on. Still I kept my friends, Armenian and Russian, in happy ignorance of my movements, and decamped one day without warning for the commercial port of the Caspian.

The journey from Tiflis to Baku is scarcely as interesting, from the point of view of scenery, as the journey from Batoum to Tiflis. Gradually the country begins to assume that flat and barren aspect which is characteristic of the shores of the Caspian and the northern plateau of the stony tableland of Asia Minor. The poor little single tramway-line which has been dignified with the grandiloquent title of the Trans-Caucasian Railway, winds its slow and tedious way at a pace that is simply exasperating.

But then the company was more interesting. One of the occupants of the compartment in which I found myself was an officer of police, the other a quaint-looking person, with an extremely intelligent cast of countenance. This gentleman had a wonderful quantity of curios with him, and being of an expansive disposition, very soon entered into conversation with us and proceeded to unpack his treasures. These he had collected wherever he had travelled, for, as he told us, he was very extravagant and was unable to keep money ; for this reason, he said, he always spent a large part of the money he took with him on a journey in the purchase of objects of antiquarian interest, and thus he flattered himself that if he was unable to keep his money he at least did not waste it. This revelation of ingenuousness was followed by a voluntary communication as to where he was at present coming from. He had been to St. Petersburg as a member of one of the deputations of the nobles of the Caucasus to do homage to the young Emperor Nicholas II. It turned out that he was an Armenian nobleman and had relations in high positions at St. Petersburg, and so his conversation was most interesting.

He told us the story of the famous speech of the Emperor to the nobles, in which all hopes of Russia's ever obtaining any measure of political freedom was completely dispelled. Here is the story, which I think bears upon it the stamp of probability; at any rate my informant could have no possible object in inventing it.

The programme of the reception had been carefully prepared. A speech from the Emperor did not figure in it. The deputations took up their position in the Hall of St. George at the Winter Palace. Each deputation was to be received separately by the Emperor and Empress in an adjoining apartment, and was then to be dismissed. In accordance with these arrangements the nobles were assembled, when Count Vorontzoff-Dashkoff, the Minister of the Court, made his appearance and announced that, before receiving the deputations separately, His Imperial Majesty wished to address a few words to them in a body. This was a departure from the programme, and put everybody on the tiptoe of expectation. Presently the Imperial body-guards took up a position in the hall. The officers of the court arrived. A long wait ensued. Messengers came and went. There were hurried consultations. Something had gone wrong. Suddenly it was announced that his Imperial Majesty had changed his mind. The body-guards were withdrawn, and the deputations were left to speculate on what might be the cause of these alterations. After the lapse of about half an hour, the large folding doors of the hall were thrown open, and on the threshold appeared the Emperor himself. In a clear ringing voice he made the famous speech which was telegraphed all over the world. It was short and was delivered in a few minutes. When His Majesty had finished speaking, he turned on his heel and was gone. Every individual member of the deputations felt himself personally insulted. At the same time the nobles thought they could see by his countenance that the Emperor recognised his mistake, even while speaking. This impression was strengthened by the way in which he afterwards received them. He was particularly cordial, conciliatory, and even apologetic in his manner. The Empress, by her grace, dignity, charm, and beauty, won the hearts of all.

What did it mean? What was the reason for this moral box on the ear to the Emperor's most loyal and devoted subjects? The mystery was soon solved.

It appears that before the announcement by Count Vorontzoff-Dashkoff was made, M. Pobedonostzeff, the Procureur of the Holy Synod, and M. Dournovo, the Minister of the Interior, insisted on seeing the Emperor, and, on being admitted to his presence, presented him with the text of the speech, solemnly impressing upon him the necessity of delivering it. The Emperor at first refused to comply, but afterwards yielded to pressure. The deputation was thereupon informed of his intention of addressing them. At this juncture the Emperor's most influential cousin, the Grand Duke Constantine Constantinovitch, succeeded in dissuading him from making his speech, and so the body-guards were withdrawn from the hall. But MM. Dournovo and Pobedonostzeff now returned to the charge, and implored the Emperor not to neglect this great opportunity of declaring his views. It is even believed that they threatened to resign if he refused. So he yielded.

Everybody will remember the speech in which the Emperor told the nobles of Russia that they must for ever banish from their minds all foolish dreams of liberty. It was provoked by a loyal address from the Zemstvo—or county council—of Tver, which was a covert petition for a constitution. But the nobles of Russia were in no way associated with this address, and came to St. Petersburg solely to do homage to their sovereign, as an act of allegiance. His unprovoked rebuke came upon them like a thunder-bolt.

The garrulous Armenian nobleman informed us that the Emperor was looking very well and robust, and was very much in love with his beautiful consort, who had already won golden opinions.

He also told us an amusing story of the Marshal of Nobility of a district in the Caucasus, which quaintly illustrates the manners of that region. This high functionary was noted for his avarice, and complained that, on his way to the railway which was to take him to St. Petersburg for the coronation, he was attacked by brigands, who robbed him of his luggage, including valuable diamonds and a very handsome new marshal's uniform, profusely decorated with gold lace. A Marshal of Nobility holds a position somewhat analogous to our Lord Lieutenants of counties. His story, received on the word of so high a functionary, had to be credited. His losses were refunded to him, and the police are still looking for the brigands, who have not, however, been found. Now it was a matter of common knowledge amongst his intimates that the Marshal had not purchased a new uniform at all, and possessed no diamonds, and it was generally believed that he had himself arranged or invented the attack by brigands.

This story was considered a very good joke, and heartily laughed at. It did not occur to the man who told it, or to the police official who was listening, that it cast a very serious reflection on the state of society in the Caucasus. The country life of Russia abounds in similar episodes.

It was now the turn of the police official to entertain us, and he proved quite as garrulous and communicative as the Armenian country gentleman. He talked about the Russo-Turkish war and General Skobeleff; but what interested me most was a piece of intelligence, which he communicated quite unsuspectingly, little dreaming of its value to me, to whom he was an absolute stranger. I was supposed to be travelling to Baku on business. So I was. It appears that this police official was the prefect or commissioner of a large district, with a population of 100,000, all Mahomedans. He complained of the extreme ignorance and stupidity of peasants. We had been discussing the remarkable phenomenon exhibited by Russia where the peasants have lately taken to emigrating to Siberia in large numbers, generally to return impoverished, often to die of want in that distant region, because the Government had very badly organised the system of allotment of land. Of course the reason why the Russian peasant emigrates is, that his life is made impossible for him at home. Of late, harvests have been bad, but taxes have to be paid. On the one hand he is ground down by the Government and its officials, on the other, by the petty tyranny of the village commune, or Mir, and the local money-lender, who is often the village elder.

The police prefect, however, developed a very curious theory. He maintained that all peasant populations were prone to emigration, an obviously false statement, and supported it by adducing a very startling fact. He stated that, in his own district, his Mahomedan population had developed a totally inexplicable fondness for emigrating, and an illogical partiality for the dominions of the Sultan. A rumour had reached them that, if they went to Turkey, land would be given them, and so they were anxious to go. It was useless to point out to them that they were much better off under Russian rule, had less taxes to pay, and enjoyed better government. These arguments would not convince them. They clamoured for permission to emigrate. It was most irrational and stupid.

Personally, I was not inclined to think that these Mahomedans were acting quite so foolishly as the police-prefect seemed to believe. On the contrary, I thought it was not unlikely that they had more substantial data to go on than mere rumours. I was therefore not surprised when the Armenian nobleman, having asked the official how long this movement had been going on, and learnt that it had developed to alarming proportions only within two years, said :

" I should not wonder if it was connected with the Armenian question."

All I can say is, no more should I. The Sultan, having determined on exterminating the Armenians, would very naturally be looking round for an industrious and wealth-producing Mahomedan population to take their place. Perhaps such a supposition is calculated to credit the Sultan with more statesmanship than we believe him possessed of ; but then, life is full of strange surprises, and the workings of the human mind are difficult to fathom.

My two travelling companions left me one by one, and I spent the night by myself in my compartment. The day had well advanced before I reached Baku.

A strange spectacle awaits you on your arrival at

this city. You see before you an enormous barren sand waste, beyond it the sea. No town is in sight. Suddenly you discover that the sand plain is the end of a plateau, and as you descend it you see the town of Baku fringing the shores of the Caspian. On your approach your nostrils become invaded by that odour of naphtha which shall never leave you until you have left Baku miles behind you.

It is a strange looking town, and would be handsome were the houses loftier. The streets are broad and clean ; there is a magnificent quay. Tramways abound. Here the telephone is in full operation, and if there was a little more bustle in the streets one might almost fancy oneself in an American city out West. There is the same air of newness about everything, the same sanguine atmosphere. Everybody is hopeful. But the quantities of Persians and Tartars in their picturesque costumes, the camels in the market-place, the Persian citadel, and the Russian peasants and soldiers, dispel the illusion. No vegetation of any kind can flourish in Baku, owing to the aridity of the soil ; but the town is enterprising, and has laid out a park. The footpaths of this park are of asphalte ; the earth in which the trees, shrubs, and flowers have been planted and pine, was brought from some more fertile region.

There are three hotels in Baku, all beyond expression vile. In one the food is less bad than in the other two, another has the best accommodation, and the third the best liquor. The division of labour is thus carried to an absurd extreme.

I was fortunate in making the acquaintance, at Tiflis, of M. Dubail, the French Vice-Consul at Baku, a gentleman of considerable parts, who had been a journalist in Paris, had gone on missions to Bulgaria, Roumania, and other places for Mr. Gordon Bennett's *New York Herald*, and who had, besides, visited North and South America. This gentleman, about thirty years of age, is leading a melancholy existence in the Russian Petrolia, and was consumedly glad of my arrival. Owing to the very defective steam-packet service across the Caspian, and unfavourable weather, I had to spend three mortal weeks at this delightful spot, and had therefore ample opportunity to study the petroleum industry of Baku.

Thanks to the courtesy of the genial representative of a sprightly nation I saw a great deal of this city, and was able to make a careful study of the life led there by the leading merchants, which resembles the life led in all the commercial towns of Russia, and may be conveniently summed up in one word—drink.

The petroleum industry is not in quite so flourishing a condition as people over here, who are unacquainted with the ways of Russian officialism, may be inclined to think.

I was taken over the largest works at Baku—I will not mention names—and found the appliances and arrangements of a very primitive order, nor was I

surprised to hear in the result that the American
Standard Oil Company was competing with the
Caucasus at its very doors, and successfully. Baku
seems to be suffering under two curses which together
are preventing her development, one is a want of
solidarity and co-operation among producers, the other
Government interference.

The principal grievance of the producers against the
Government is its refusal to construct, or allow anybody else to construct, a pipe from Baku to Batoum
for the direct delivery of the oil to the tank steamers.
That is a very great grievance. The Government is
actuated by curiously mixed motives.

In the first place it does not wish the small producer
to disappear and be swallowed up by the eventual
monopolist. For the small producer is at the mercy
of the Government, the monopolist may become too
powerful for it. Besides, the Government pretends to
foster minor industries, and to encourage the small
man, and further it adheres to the socialistic theory
that the monopolist is always an extortioner, who
sucks the life-blood of the people.

These ideas are very altruistic and have a rosy
colour, but they cannot prevail. Already the petroleum
industry of Baku is virtually in the hands of two
monopolists, the Nobel Syndicate, and the Rothschild
Syndicate, and the minor producers are all more or
less pledged either to them or to what I must call
petroleum-sweaters, for want of a better term—capi-

talists in short. Whether many abuses would not be removed and the quality of the oil greatly improved by permitting the formation of a great oil trust is hardly a question. But this the Government do not wish, as we shall see.

Another argument which is urged against the construction of a pipe is that the railway lives on its petroleum carriage, and that to take that away would mean ruination to the railway. This argument is not sound either, because if the petroleum industry was to receive a great stimulus, the wealth of the whole region would grow enormously, new industries would spring into being, and the Trans-Caucasian Railway would participate in the increased trade and the general prosperity.

But it is this general prosperity of the Caucasus which the Government is preventing by its venal officials and blindness.

The real reason, however, why the Government do not wish to see the oil-wells of Baku developed to too great an extent, is that they do not wish to encourage the production of refined petroleum, but are very anxious to secure an abundant and cheap supply of the low grade oil called "ostatki," upon which they depend for fuel for their steamers on the Caspian, and their locomotives on the Trans-Caspian and the Trans-Caucasian Railways. In other words, if you allow monopolists to get the petroleum into their hands, or if you develop the petroleum industry to such an extent as to drive out the competition of America, you run the risk of raising the price of the ostatki, and that the Government do not wish to do.

There is yet another factor in the Russian commercial policy which must not be forgotten, and this is the "industrial region of Moscow," as Russian economists call it. The great manufacturers in and around Moscow do not wish to see industrial centres springing up within the confines of the Empire. They even wish to be protected against the competition of Poland! And as they are wealthy and powerful and St. Petersburg is near, they are able to bring their influence to bear in an irresistible manner on the higher officials of the State.

There are mines and works in the Caucasus going to rack and ruin for want of capitalists to develop or undertake them. One particular ironworks comes to my mind in this connection. The company to whom the works belonged were promised a railway. That railway was never built. Another railway was built instead which left them out in the cold. They have gone bankrupt, and successively have these ironworks caused the ruin of numerous individuals and companies. There is some fatality about every industrial undertaking on the Caucasus.

But this has been a long digression. Let me illustrate the way the petroleum industry is baulked, by an incident which came under my personal observation.

A gentleman of great commercial shrewdness took me one day to see a petroleum fountain situated to the south of Baku on the Baïloff promontory. Here an exceptionally good naphtha had been found. My friend took me over the primitive works, and then showed me some waste land adjoining. "That land," he said, "is exactly of the same sort as the land on which the neighbouring oil-works are built. It is waste and idle, but I have reason to believe that oil of quite as good a quality as that produced in its vicinity could be found underneath it. I wanted to purchase this land, but it is impossible. The land belongs to the Admiralty, and they will not part with it."

This astonished me considerably, for in its present condition the land could not possibly be of any benefit to the Admiralty; it was at a considerable distance from the sea, unsuitable for stores or barracks, and close to inflammable oil-works!

My friend declined to explain the mystery. It was not until I returned to London and met a Russian gentleman who had had considerable experience with Russian officials that the mystery was cleared up. In conversation over the commercial possibilities of the Caucasus I mentioned this incident. He laughed and said :

"Don't you know why that was?"

"No," I replied. "I cannot understand the motives of the Government."

"The Government had nothing to do with the

matter ; I had a similar experience, and know exactly how these things are managed. A friend of mine wanted to purchase some land in the same way, which belonged to the Government. What happened? The clerk through whom the petition had to pass was appointed by his chief to report upon the land. He requested permission to call at his chief's private residence, and came the same evening. 'Well, what is it?' his chief enquired. 'That land, sir, is very good. It is a pity to sell it now. Let us wait, sir, until you are the head of the office and I am your assistant, and then we can sell the land and make something out of the transaction. For the present, I should think it would be more advisable to say that the department sees no advantage in selling the land ! ' This, I am quite sure, is what occurred at Baku also. But I will give you another instance of the public spirit of our officials. In a part of Siberia, the province of Yennisseisk, a Russian merchant, Buikoff by name, discovered a spring of pure naphtha which was running to waste into the Yennissei. He applied for permission to acquire this land, foolishly giving his reason. The petition was put before the Governor of the province. That important functionary flew into a violent passion, abused his underlings roundly, and told them there was no petroleum in his province. ' But, your Excellency, there can be no doubt that Mr. Buikoff is quite right,' his Secretary replied ; ' we have had the plans inspected and find that there are,

M

indeed, petroleum springs there.' 'You are all of you
a parcel of fools,' the Governor-General cried, beside
himself with rage. 'We are all living here very
comfortably, are we not? We are all making money
in a modest way, are we not? We may get promoted
in time, and get sent to St. Petersburg, and live in
luxury. And here you come with your foolish
petroleum. If petroleum wells are opened up we
shall have engineers and lawyers and all sorts of
clever people here, and we shall no longer be able to
live. Tear up all those reports and do not let me
hear another word about it.' That is how we are
governed, my dear sir."

This gentleman was not a Nihilist or a refugee, but
a prosperous merchant.

One of the features of Baku is its celebrated tower,
Keez-Kala, erected by a Khan to humour a whim of
his daughter's, who subsequently threw herself into
the sea from the top. This tower has recently been
painted a gloomy black, and I was told the reason
was that an official wanted to make some money out
of the paint.

Baku is divided into two towns, the white and the
black. In the black town are the oil refineries; it is
separated by an enormous sandy waste about five
miles in extent from Baku proper, the white town,
and is built entirely of wood, so that if it should burn,
as it often does, no valuable materials would be
wasted. Shortly before I arrived at Baku a very

handsome arcade in the white town had been completely gutted. I was edified to learn that the
building was not insured, and that the stall-holders
had lost enormously.

The most prolific oil region in the neighbourhood
of Baku is the district of Balakhanui. I was conducted over this place by M. Despot-Zenovitch,
former Mayor of Baku. To his ability and energy
Baku owes what measure of prosperity it has achieved,
and he is one of the few public-spirited men in this
arid region.

At Balakhanui the visitor will be surprised to find
enormous, almost illimitable, lakes, and still more
astonished to learn that these lakes are composed of
petroleum. All over the district are quaint pyra-
midical timber structures, like gigantic windmills
without sails. These are fountains. Occasionally a
fountain will be too impetuous for such control, and
will burst the bands of the timber structure. I have
seen such fountains spouting forth dense black
naphtha a hundred feet high, and thus forming
naphtha lakes around them. Such fountains of course
make the fortunes of their lucky owners while they
last; but they are very capricious in their behaviour,
and will stop as suddenly as they start. While they
are spouting the proprietor is the popular hero of the
day. He is photographed, fêted, pointed out in the
street. He is a celebrity, and all because he has been
lucky enough to strike oil. While he is sitting in his

club, drinking champagne and playing cards, his fountain is patiently working for him and vomiting forth from the bowels of the earth a fabulous wealth, which keeps on increasing day by day, without any effort of his, and then unexpectedly fails.

Sometimes these fountains take fire, and then the conflagration is terrible.

Not far from Balakhanui is Sourakhani, the Mecca of the fire-worshippers, with its marvellous temple of eternal fire, to which pilgrimages are yet made annually by the disciples of Zoroaster.

Baku has a population of 110,000, and exports annually about nine thousand million pounds of petroleum. The largest part of this industry is in the hands of Tartars—illiterate millionaires—of whom the Russians are in sufficient terror. There is besides a large floating Persian population, and seven per cent. of the inhabitants of the province of Baku, including the Transcaspian district of Linkoran, are Armenians. The Mahomedans form seventy-six per cent. of the population, and the Russians proper do not constitute more than three or four per cent.

The life of the merchants and officials is one continued orgy. They begin to get drunk in the morning, and continue in that state until the small hours. Consequently people do not live to a great age, but are old and decrepit at fifty. There are no other amusements. Some interesting data regarding the condition of the drama in Russia will be gathered from a perusal

of the ' Baku Annual,' published by Mishon, an Armenian photographer. Thus, in deploring the absence
of a permanent theatre, the Annual states that
managers are discouraged from visiting Baku by
the apathy of the public and the expenses inseparable
from all theatrical enterprises. " Every one knows,"
says the Annual, " that the remuneration of dramatic
artists, and of all theatrical employees, which managers
have to give is much higher than in any other pro-
fession. It is not unusual for the monthly salaries of
the interpreters of leading parts to vary from 250 to
400 roubles (£25–40), while actors of a secondary
category receive as much as from 60 to 150 roubles
(£6–15) a month." The Annual thereupon makes
an estimate of the expenses of management and
arrives at the conclusion that a season costs a
manager as much as four hundred pounds a month.

This shows how very moderate salaries are, and
how very little enterprise there must be at Baku.

A perusal of the various accessible documents from
which it is possible to obtain anything approaching to
a trustworthy statement of the resources and prosperity of Baku is melancholy. Education is in a bad
state, trade is languishing, the petroleum is kept down
by American competition and other causes. The
recreations of the people may be summarised in the
three words drunkenness, debauchery, and murder.
Such is the unflattering picture of the social and
economic condition of Baku.

Needless to say that here there has been very little display of that national Armenian spirit which is so strongly developed in Tiflis under the very eyes of the authorities. For all that there has been a wonderful amount of money bestowed to the Armenian cause by the wealthy Armenian merchants of this city, who, by the way, are among the least debauched of its inhabitants.

But much of this money has found its way into the pockets of dishonest persons, and so there is some hesitation to contribute more. Nevertheless, public subscriptions are still kept up; charity balls and concerts are given. On the whole, however, the spirit of Baku is commercial and oleaginous; there is little room for altruistic emotion.

CHAPTER IX.

AT last, after three weeks of unprofitable trifling at Baku, I got on board the *Grand-Duke Constantine*, and started for my trip across the Caspian. The steamers run once a fortnight. They are owned by a company, but are officered and manned by naval reserve men, and form virtually part of the Russian transport service. There are about six of them, and they average 600 tons, if as much. They might be turned into very comfortable yachts if they were properly fitted, and had new engines put into them ; but in their present state they are indescribably dirty, alive with every possible kind of vermin, and have miserable engines, which shake them nearly to pieces at every revolution, although their average speed does not exceed six knots an hour. The Admiralty House and naval barracks at Baku are very extensive ; there must be at least three thousand men quartered in those commodious buildings, which are larger than any ordinary German military barracks, and constitute a little separate town on the Baïloff promontory. But there are no ships! Of course there are one or two gun-boats; but how, in the event of a descent on India or Persia, Russia is to pour her troops over the miserable Caucasian tramway, in rickety little steamers across the Caspian, and then over another single line of tramway through Central Asia, is a puzzle. Nobody in his senses, who has studied the question, can believe that Russia would ever become a serious menace to England, provided England does not allow herself to be bullied and bluffed into a position which would put her at a great disadvantage.

Anybody who has the vaguest general acquaintance with military matters, knows that a modern army of 100,000 or so takes something to move and transport. But if we cast a glance over the melancholy spectacle of the Trans-Caucasian Railway, with its innumerable truck-waggons standing on sidings all along the road, waiting to be transported to Batoum, where their advent is being greedily awaited by the tank-steamers which will take the oil to the markets of the world, we shall understand that, if commerce cannot stimulate this railway into activity, it is hopeless to expect it to render any effective service in the hour of national emergency or danger.

Russia has about 100,000 regular troops on the Caucasus, the Volga is practically denuded of soldiers, and she can ill spare many men from the Black Sea ports. All her strength is concentrated on the German and Austrian frontiers; such troops as she

can spare from Poland she has massed in St. Petersburg, Moscow, and Kieff.

But supposing her to be engaged in a war with
Persia or in Central Asia, she would have to send
her supplies from her nearest centre, and that is the
Black Sea.

From Odessa, Nikolaieff, and Sevastopol she might
be able to fit out an expeditionary army. This army
would have to be transported across the Caucasus, over
the Caspian, and be compelled to travel very slowly.

The Russians are thoroughly alive to the weakness
of their Caucasian link. It is their most vulnerable
point.

My wretched little steamer, with its horrible smell
of naphtha, its filthy cabins, the berths in which were
even unprovided with sheets, took about three days to
get to Enzeli, the Persian port.

She rolled and vibrated horribly, and stopped at
innumerable little stations, all of which received contributions from amongst our passengers, who turned
out to be chiefly officials of the Government. There
was a small sprinkling of Armenian commercial
travellers, fierce, hardy-looking men, the pioneers
of Russian trade, who spoke, besides their native
language, Russian, Turkish, Persian, and often Tartar
and Greek. There was also a Belgian merchant, an
extraordinarily enterprising man, who had established
a depôt at Enzeli, and traded in everything. He had
some excellent Caucasian brandy, of which I bought

a dozen bottles, and very glad I was of it afterwards, and he also made me buy a Belgian fowling-piece with cartridges, for which I was very grateful, and which I subsequently sold on my return journey. Two other individuals aroused my suspicions, they were Greeks ; one, a Greek merchant who had a large store at Resht, and was going to develop the silk industry in Persia. Another, also a Greek, but from Constantinople, who pretended that he, likewise, was bent on cocoons, but who let out to me in confidence, that he was on the staff of the *Moniteur Oriental,* the agent of the Turkish Foreign Office, and who subsequently disappeared most mysteriously. His very strange conduct during his stay at Resht led me to believe that he was really a Turkish spy.

At length we reached Enzeli ; but there is a bar at Enzeli, and the Russian steamers are unable to cross it. Consequently it is usual to fetch the passengers in a small steam tender, which is kept at Enzeli for the purpose. Occasionally, however, the breakers passing over the bar are so dangerous that the tender refuses to come out. Then enterprising boatmen in quaint barges, like viking ships, and entirely flat-bottomed, sally forth. There are times, however, when even these deem the sea too dangerous. Then the steamer waits for the sea to go down. If it does not go down in forty-eight hours, the steamer returns to Baku without delivering its cargo, and one has to wait another fortnight for a fresh steamer, when it is quite possible that a similar fate will be in store for one. On this occasion a fierce storm was raging, the rain was descending, the wind was blowing its hardest, and the dirty little *Constantine* was riding at anchor, rolling and tossing about in the most absurd manner. The passengers all looked pitiable objects. For myself, I was in despair, for the captain told me cheerfully that he expected the storm would last, and that we should be unable to land.

Presently the rain stopped, and we were able to see the palace of the Shah in the distance and the little steam-launch, which ought to have come out to fetch us, but would not, lying snug and comfortable in the harbour or bay.

The palace of the Shah was a strange-looking structure in the shape of a tower, white, picked out with blue, and looking like some gigantic piece of crockery-ware. The Shah has no authority in the Caspian, where he may not even fly his flag. I was told later by our Consul at Resht, Mr. Churchill, that when the late Shah paid his last visit to Europe and crossed the Caspian to Baku in his yacht, a Russian gunboat threatened to open fire on him if he did not hoist down his standard. He was reluctantly compelled to obey ; but the Russian flag may be seen flying insolently at Enzeli.

We remained at anchor for twenty-four mortal hours, tossed about by the surging waves. On the following morning we found ourselves surrounded by small craft ; and a Russian courier, an officer of Cossacks, came on board. He looked pale and emaciated and in a terrible state of fear when he staggered into our saloon cabin. He had come direct from Teheran and reported the roads to be in a fearful condition. His orderly, a fine, tall young fellow, had sunk exhausted on his master's saddle-bags and fallen incontinently to sleep. This was a pleasant foretaste of what was in store for me !

The Greek merchant, who had a store at Resht and spoke very good French, offered me a seat in his boat on my proposing to share expenses with him, and my luggage was thrown in. By a sheer miracle I succeeded in getting into his boat, and we were soon rowing off to shore, pulled by the most villainous-looking crew I ever set eyes on. They were half naked, and looked starved and wretched, but extremely ferocious. I learned that these unfortunate men were engaged by a contractor, who was himself employed by another contractor, and that they got a very small share of the profits. So that even in Persia sweating exists. Some of them had the most repulsive sores on their bare arms and legs, and they were certainly not a decent spectacle for a lady to look at. Fortunately there were no ladies with us, and, indeed, European ladies are rarely met with travelling in Persia.

Instead of taking the breakers nose on, as I expected we should, we took the bar broadside on,

and were gently washed over, though how we managed
to escape being upset is beyond my comprehension.
After long and toilsome pulling we at last made the
bay of Enzeli, and a beautiful spectacle unfolded itself
before us. In front of us lay the expansive waters of
the Murghab, a large freshwater lake opening on to
the sea. In the background were beautiful forests,
snow-capped mountains, and the water was fringed
with that rich vegetation which is characteristic of
marshy land. On our right was the inconceivably
quaint palace of the Shah, with the bazaars and
picturesque wooden buildings of Enzeli farther on.
On our left was the Persian custom-house, with the
hotel, kept by an Armenian of course, and the
store-houses of the steamboat company. Farther
on were the fishermen's huts of another Armenian
merchant, who had the fishing of the Murghab.

The sky had cleared up, and was of an intense blue,
and the air was alive with birds and water-fowl of
every description. I quite fell in love with Persia
on this my first introduction to it.

The custom-house authorities had not yet arrived,
and so we had once more to row across the Murghab
to fetch them out of the town of Enzeli and bring
them back. The noise and shouting that went on
were perfectly demoniacal. Fortunately I had little
trouble with the officials, my papers were in order;
but I had to pay an extortionate fee for the dirty
Persian stamp and its curious hieroglyphics which

were affixed. My Greek friend had a different fortune, and spent about an hour in a terrific swearing match, in which he was pitted apparently against the entire population of Enzeli, but seemed to come off with flying colours. I did not understand a word of what he said, but was immensely impressed by his language, and feel confident that it would have completely collapsed any able-bodied English bargee had it been literally translated.

This part of the business done, we got into our boat again and rowed peacefully up the Murghab towards Pir Bazaar, the port of the Murghab and the commercial outpost of Resht. The journey in the boat was delightful. We refreshed the inner man with Muscovite beer, a kind of sour cream cheese, and flaps of thin, flabby bread, which looked like flannel doilies.

But on our arrival at Pir Bazaar my martyrdom commenced. The bazaar was in charge of an Armenian clerk, who was reading a revolutionary Armenian paper published at Marseilles, and was deep in "atrocities." The building was an island in a sea of mud, knee deep. Everything was covered with mud, our luggage, our clothes, horses and carts, and everything seemed to be alive with vermin.

I have never anywhere seen such mud as I saw at Pir Bazaar; it was wonderful, thick, succulent, black, boggy. One sank into it at every step, and there seemed no refuge from it—it was all pervasive.

On the journey by boat I noticed numerous
flamingoes, herons, storks, and similar birds, and as
we got more inland, and left the magnificent lake
behind us with its glorious mountain scenery, we
approached a country which strongly reminded me
of the smiling green fields and underwood which
skirt our own Thames. On the banks I saw grazing
the quaint little Persian bulls with humps on their
backs. These humps, by the way, are very good
eating, and when salted resemble tongue. Here,
also, are the tobacco-fields for which Enzeli is famous.

The fishing of the Murghab is farmed by the
ubiquitous Armenians of the Caucasus.

I performed the journey from Pir Bazaar to Resht
in a conveyance resembling a victoria, and not unlike
the hooded droshkis familiar to the traveller who has
been to Moscow. The horse was harnessed in the
Russian fashion, with a bow, or "douga," over its neck.
I was surprised to see that all the cart-horses which I
met on the road were harnessed in a similar manner.
Trifling details often produce general impressions,
and, what with the Russian Armenian clerks at Pir
Bazaar, the Russian droshka, the Russian flag waving
on the Murghab, I felt that, although I had left Russia
behind me, I was still within the sphere of Russian
influence, and that here at least Russia was synony-
mous with civilisation. At Pir Bazaar the Armenian
clerk in charge had a Russian samovar !

My Greek friend, with whom I parted company at

Pir Bazaar, recommended me the only hotel Resht could boast of, kept by a Greek also, and told me that the road from Pir Bazaar to Resht had been recently mended for the passage of General Kurapatkin, the Russian special envoy to Teheran.

It is a fine road about four miles long, straight and broad, but paved with cobbles. These cobbles had sunk into the soil in parts, and here and there enormous ditches had been formed. Over these cobbles had been strewn in a loose, careless way, and this was what was called repairing the road. I fervently wished it had been left in its original state. Never shall I forget the horrors of that drive to Resht. The sea voyage was nothing to it. It was drizzling most depressingly, and we bumped about in a terrific manner, while I held on to my baggage with the tenacity of despair, feeling that if one of my packages were to tumble into the slough of despond beneath me, I should never be able to fish it out again. Nearly every bone in my body was bruised by the time I got to Resht. It was heart-rending to see the carts and pack-horses laden with goods which we met on the way. Bales of cotton, pieces of machinery, all manner of merchandise lay scattered about on the road, firmly embedded in the mud, and covered with slimy filth.

Enzeli is the only port of Persia in the Caspian, and Resht the first town of importance on the way to Teheran. Yet, notwithstanding the undoubted influence of Russia, the port is in a pitiable condition. We have seen how difficult of access it is by sea. The arm of the Murghab, which runs to Pir Bazaar, is so shallow that steamers cannot navigate it. A small steam launch does run to the mouth of this narrow inlet, but here its cargo has to be transhipped and put into primitive boats, which are rowed and towed to Pir Bazaar. Why a tramway has not been laid from Pir Bazaar to Resht is beyond my comprehension; but if the Russians are supine, the Persians are apathetic. The population do not seem to live, they appear to be in a state of suspended animation.

Much has been said about the picturesqueness of Persian costume. Of this I am compelled to say I saw no traces among the peasantry. They were clothed in rags, which might have belonged originally to Italian lazzaroni, Irish beggars, or anybody. Whatever their colour might once have been, they were of a uniform neutral tint, and could only be described as filthily dirty. The people who wore them looked like scarecrows with horribly emaciated faces, all skin and bones. Nowhere have I ever seen more pitiable objects. I had been told that the Persians were very fanatical, but I thought they looked more like famished wild beasts than dangerous fanatics, and seemed to regard me more with fear than hatred. As I got to know more of the country, I came to the conclusion that the Persians were much more intelligent and cultured than the Turks, though they

N

had, of course, fewer opportunities of rubbing
shoulders with Europeans. By culture I must not
be understood to mean familiarity with Western
civilisation, but native culture, the indigenous culture
of their own peculiar institutions, and I found them
brighter, more intelligent, more sympathetic and
imaginative than the moribund Turks.

If a country is to be judged by its form of government, then Persia is indeed hopelessly backward. In
my journey through Turkey, Russia, and Persia, I
came upon three degrees of despotism. The civilised
European despotism of Russia, presenting a social
organism still very rudimentary in form, but more
highly developed than the semi-barbarous Turkey,
where despotism is hideous, but where the government
is nevertheless vertebrate. In Persia, however, we
have an entirely rudimentary and invertebrate form
of government, the lowest type of an Oriental despotism. The government is divided up among local
satraps, who again have satraps under them ; the taxes
are farmed, and the people are afraid of showing any
outward signs of prosperity lest they should lose what
little property they have. They bury their treasure,
and even their corn and flour, and go about half-naked.
The bastinado is the common form of punishment, and
nobody is exempt—not even members of the Imperial
family. Mutilations are common. Thieves are
punished by having their right hands cut off. Feet
are cut off ; the tongue is pulled out. But for all that

the bastinado is the usual form of punishment, and is
less barbarous than one is inclined to believe. Of course,
to be beaten on the naked soles of the feet is very painful, and sometimes as many as five hundred blows are
administered, the recipient being crippled for life. It
is not at all uncommon for the toes to fall off after
excessive punishment, and the pain is always so acute
that the nervous system receives a severe shock from
which, in the case of sensitive subjects, it never re-
covers. But these are extreme cases, and on the
whole the bastinado, though a very painful, is not a
very inhuman form of punishment. For instance,
under its infliction people do not bleed to death.
Though toes may drop off, the entire body is not
ruined. Take, on the other hand, the results of
punishment with a cat-o'-nine tails. It is not so many
years ago that soldiers in this country received as many
as five hundred lashes with this fiendish instrument of
torture. It was generally considered that a soldier
who had been flogged was unfitted for active service,
and he was generally discharged a broken-down, ruined
man. Many men have died under the lash, or in
consequence of a flogging. In the navy, punishment
was, if possible, more brutal still, and the custom of
flogging a man through the fleet was simply barbarous.
In Russia, the pleyt is a terrible form of punishment,
which is still, I believe, administered in rare instances
in Siberia. It is not ten years ago that a woman was
flogged to death in Siberia.

N 2

Running the gauntlet in the Prussian army was not a mild form of punishment either. I made numerous inquiries while I was in Persia, and could not hear of a single case of a man having been bastinadoed to death ; and when once the soles are healed the person who has suffered punishment is as well as he was before. Of course in administering the bastinado, as in every other form of corporal punishment, everything depends upon the executioner. He is frequently bribed to spare the culprit, and lay on his blows gently. And here I may say by way of parenthesis that bribery is as rampant in Persia as in Turkey.

But to continue my journey. More dead than alive I arrived at Resht, and was driven to the hostelry of the Greek, which looked into a very pretty garden with a fountain in the middle, and was exactly like a house taken bodily out of the Arabian Nights. I was led up some curious stairs, which were really outside the house, and made of large stones ; so high were the steps that it was an effort to ascend them. I was then shown into a spacious room, with Oriental ornaments in stucco, an elaborate system of curtains, and no furniture beyond an iron bedstead, a rickety table, and a couple of chairs. In this room I spent three weeks of my life. The walls were whitewashed, and the whitewash came off on one's clothes on going incautiously near them.

I was very hungry, and so dinner was served in the

common dining-room, an equally gorgeous apartment with very little furniture. The food was coarse but not bad; but the famous Persian wine was disgusting.

I spent my evening taking my ease at mine inn, and chatting with the Greek commercial travellers who were staying there, among them being the venerable gentleman who was pretending to be interested in cocoons, but had confided to me that he was the correspondent of the *Moniteur Oriental* of Constantinople, usually called the *Menteur Oriental*, or Oriental Liar.

The next day I proceeded, escorted by a guide, to the house of the English Consul, Mr. Churchill. The road lay through the best part of the town, which seemed to consist entirely of bazaars, and reminded me of nothing so much as of an enormous country fair. The road was muddy, irregular, and narrow; but the people were a great sight. The distinctive note of the people of Resht is their extreme emaciation, pallor, and suppleness of figure. Their faces are intensely intelligent, though long and narrow; but there is a fire in their eyes which the Turk lacks altogether. The Turks always seemed to me to be only partially re-animated corpses.; the Persians looked like evil genii. Of course, everybody knows the usual costume of the Persian, his long peaked cap, and his long cloak or caftan, as well as the green turban and coat of the Sayed, or son of the Prophet, of whom there are, it is needless to say, great quantities. But what struck me about the costumes of these Frenchmen of the East, as they are called most appropriately, for they are certainly most courteous and polished, was the wonderful way in which they harmonised their colours. Blues, greens, yellows, browns, and drabs prevailed ; but there were no discordant colours, and bright reds seemed to be eschewed. Quietness was the prevailing tone, though of course this quietness invariably vanished whenever Persian met Persian over a bargain. Then the yells and shrieks were something blood-curdling, one would have thought that the people were murdering each other, to hear them.

The emaciated appearance of the people was due to the fact that the great Mahomedan fast of the Rhamazan was being solemnised, and the faithful followers of the Prophet during this period are not allowed to touch food from sunset to sunrise. In revenge they turn night into a veritable saturnalia. The women of Persia dress much more gracefully than those of Turkey. They generally wear a kind of loose black bournous of alpaca, with dainty bloomers, terminating in exquisitely pretty little shoes. Over their heads they wear a kind of hood, from which is suspended a white veil which hangs down, and is provided with a couple of eyelets, from which they can peep at the stranger. Their general appearance is that of the members of some Roman Catholic Sisterhood.

When we had at last got out of the bazaar and proceeded through what I suppose was the town proper, I was surprised to see with what regardlessness to plan the houses had been grouped. Indeed, the fashionable part of Resht, which is a town with a population of 100,000, although the gazetteers do not accord it more than 35,000, can only be described as a colony of houses, fortuitously grouped together, not a city. There is a Governor, and there are officials ; but the place looks like a huge village with a fair in the centre. Trees and plots of green grass abound, for vegetation is abundant, and the general aspect of the country reminds one of a sort of wild England. Private houses stand in their own grounds and are surrounded by gardens and courtyards, which are enclosed in stern, forbidding walls, as is indeed the custom in most Oriental countries.

Mr. Churchill, who has spent the best part of his life in Persia, speaks and writes Persian like a native, and has married the daughter of Dr. Tolozon, the Body-Physician of the late Shah, received me with the greatest hospitality. He apologised for not being able to put me up, but explained that in his little cottage—it is indeed little more—there was no room or the reception of visitors. He nevertheless insisted upon my spending my days and taking my meals with him, and used regularly to have me escorted home, mounted on one of his horses, by his chief cavasse, a colonel of artillery, or " topchee," as he was called. He also introduced me to his Russian colleague, who was lodged in a veritable palace, had a guard of honour of—I think it was twelve—mounted Cossacks, a vice-consul, a clerk, and a regular consular staff, so that his household represented a small Russia in Persia. He was a most amiable and charming man, and gave a dinner in my honour, to which he invited the entire European colony of Resht, the Governor, several local dignitaries, the Ahmid es Sultaneh, Governor of Talish, and several Armenians, who were the only Russian subjects under his care.

It was at Resht that I heard of General Koura-patkin's report. Of his mission the whole of the Caucasus was full; but his secret report to the Emperor, on his return to St. Petersburg from Teheran, was new to me. In this document I learned that he recommended the construction of a harbour at Enzeli, the laying down a railway from Pir Bazaar to Resht, and continuing it from Resht to Teheran; but this was only one part of his scheme. While the line Enzeli-Resht-Teheran was in progress, another line was to be constructed, from Kars to Erivan, Julfa, Tabreez, and Teheran, this line to be ultimately continued to Bushire. Meshed was also to be connected with the Transcaspian line. These schemes are not new. Some five years ago or more the Russian Consul-General of Tabreez wrote a secret report to his Government on the conquest of Persia, in which he recommended a very similar programme, and is stated to have expressed the opinion that one regiment of Cossacks would suffice to conquer the whole of Persia ; and, indeed, the Persians I saw did not strike me as very warlike.

In Mr. Churchill's house I saw and read Mr Curzon's remarkably compendious book on Persia, and was grieved to find that that statesman had been so impressed by the growth of the influence of Russia in Northern Persia that he considered it hopeless for England and English trade to attempt to recover lost ground. Mr. Curzon seems to think that the inevitable must be faced, and that in the not distant future England will have to limit her sphere of influence to Southern Persia, while resigning the north to Russia. How little this is likely to content that country General Kourapatkin's report shows. Russia longs to get to the Persian Gulf, and there are not wanting English politicians who would be inclined to humour her.

During my stay at Resht, and during my journey through Persia, I was impressed at least with one fact, and that was the remarkable hold which Russia seems to have got on the trade of the country. The Russian *samovar*, or hot-water urn, is in use in every Persian family. Everybody drinks tea, and the tea is imported from Russia. All imports of value come across the Caucasus : Russian furniture, Russian cotton manufactures, Russian boots, Russian harnesses

—in short, quantities of Russian manufactures for daily use abound. The fishing trade is practically a Russian monopoly. Against this invasion of Russian commerce the Imperial Bank of Persia is the only counterbalancing factor on the side of Great Britain. It has a hard battle to fight against Russian influence, but it is doing so bravely and with a certain measure of success. Still Russia looks with disfavour on all enterprise that is not of a Russian source, and I was told that it was for this reason that the port of Enzeli was in such a disgraceful state, and that Pir Bazaar was still unconnected by railway with Resht. On several occasions Belgian and other capitalists had obtained concessions for these and other public works, but their concessions had always lapsed, and nothing had come of the undertakings, thanks to the active hostility of Russia.

To all practical intents and purposes Persia is already a Russian Protectorate, and English influence is a mere cipher in that country.

With the object of facilitating my journey to Tabreez, where my Armenian friends in Tiflis had told me I should find bold and determined people who would convey me across the frontier to Van, from whence it would be easy to get to Bitlis and Moosh, Mr. Churchill introduced me to the Ahmid es Sultaneh, a powerful nobleman, the Governor of Talish, and the feudal lord of a fine body of cavalry recruited from the hills. In any case, I should have to ride through his territory, and so Mr. Churchill thought I had better do so as his guest.

This great noble, a wiry mountaineer, as hard as nails, received me with true Oriental politeness, and in the course of conversation I hinted that Russia was waiting for Persia to fall into her lap like a ripe apple.

The wily Oriental smiled, nodded and agreed with this opinion. I thereupon hinted that I thought Persia should lose no time in making herself strong, and in preparing to resist invasion. He shook his head, and told me there was no occasion for that; Persia need not trouble about Russia, because England would never forsake her, and would never allow her to fall a prey to Russia. "And Russia," he added significantly, "is afraid of your big guns."

This is in a nutshell the political philosophy of Persia. It is no use bothering about resisting Russia because England will not allow her to go too far; but in the meantime Russia is slowly and firmly encircling Persia in her affectionate embrace.

The Ahmid es Sultaneh readily promised to receive me as his guest, offered to make me a present of a horse, and promised me an escort. All along the journey I was to be lodged at his houses and palaces, and in short, I was to have a good time.

Unfortunately the weather was beginning to break, and the rainy season threatened to set in. The Ahmid es Sultaneh had to issue instructions for my reception.

I had to make preparations for my journey, and lay in a stock of provisions, besides purchasing travelling requisites, such as a saddle and bridle, a Persian abbah, a cloak of camel's hair, through which neither rain nor cold can penetrate, saddle-bags, and numerous other articles. All these I got with the aid of Mr. Churchill's youngest brother, a youngster of eighteen, boiling over with life and energy, whom his brother lent me to act as my interpreter during the journey.

We made several false starts, and were driven back by the unpreparedness of the Ahmid es Sultaneh's men ; but at last, after waiting three weeks in Resht, I finally started, having previously entertained, by way of a joke, Mr. Churchill and his family at dinner at my little inn, for mine host had discovered a couple of bottles of champagne, and I wanted to surprise the English Consul.

CHAPTER X.

IN a deluge of rain, and escorted by Mr. and Mrs. Churchill, young Churchill, a scamp of a servant, also lent me by Mr. Churchill, a Greek merchant, and a pack horse, we started for Pir Bazaar. There we ound our old friend the Armenian clerk still reading his Armenian paper, published at Marseilles, a new number, let us hope, for I had spent three weeks at Resht ; and I took leave of our hospitable Consul and jumped into the primitive flat-bottomed tub provided for me, and, accompanied by young Churchill and our servant, was rowed off to Enzeli.

It had been decided that, as the rivers were much swollen by the rains, I should ride along the shores of the Caspian, stopping in the houses of the Ahmid es Sultaneh on the way, to Astara, where I should be passed on to the Governor of that place, who in turn would pass me on to the Governor of Ardabil, from whence I was to proceed to Tabreez.

I should not forget to mention that the Greek gentleman, who had told me that he was the co respondent of the *Moniteur Oriental*, had left Resht, and had returned to Enzeli, ostensibly to look after some merchandise which he was expecting. At Enzeli I discovered that no merchandise had arrived for him, but that he had returned by steamer to Baku. I also learned from the English Consul that this honest Greek merchant had called on the Governor of Resht, and had reported to him that I was a suspicious character and ought to be sent back to Baku. The Governor made inquiries of Mr. Churchill, and having ascertained that I was going to visit the English Consul at Tabreez, and was meanwhile to be the guest of the Ahmid es Sultaneh, felt that he could not take any notice of the officious action of the correspondent of the *Moniteur Oriental*, who returned to his native country probably with his mission unfulfilled. But that the Turkish Government was carefully shadowing me I had reason to know at Tabreez. That, however, is advancing matters.

When we arrived at Enzeli, dined on the veranda of the Armenian hotel, and lighted our pipes with some excellent English contraband tobacco, which I had taken the precaution of buying in Constantinople, both young Churchill and myself felt that we were something like sucking Stanleys, and had an adventurous journey to look forward to. It was a beautiful evening ; before us under the veranda lay the wide expanse of the Murghab, opposite the town of Enzeli proper, with the remarkable palace of the

Shah, where, by the bye, Mr. Churchill was born, and here and there a light reflected on the water. .

Presently we were approached by an emissary of Ahmid es Sultaneh, who came to receive our orders as to when and where we should like to have our horses, so at least he said. As a matter of fact he came to tell us what the programme was that had been arranged for us, and we very soon discovered that this programme would have to be very strictly adhered to if we did not wish our escort to " eat the stick," as the poetical Persians say. For in Persia the verb to eat is used very loosely and vaguely. Thus, when a man falls he is said to " eat the earth," when he is drowned he " eats the water " ; in short, it would seem that there was nothing that an able-bodied Persian could not eat.

As we sat on our veranda, gazing on the stars and into the darkness, we could hear in the distance, and proceeding from the other side of the Murghab, an uncanny sound of barking.

" Those are the jackals. If you hear them replying from the other side it means that we shall have a fine day to-morrow," said Churchill.

But they did not reply.

The next morning we started in a boat for our point of departure. ¡We were told this was distant only about three hours from Enzeli, and we were soon sailing merrily along the Murghab. Presently a pretty fresh breeze sprung up, the breeze stiffened into a mild sort of squall, and our boatmen insisted on putting back. Hitherto I had meekly acquiesced in everything ; but I was not going to waste another day at Enzeli, and so I managed to make myself most unmistakeably understood, and we did not put back, but we lost our way ! It was not till midnight that we reached our destination a small village in the territory of the Ahmid es Sultaneh. We went through a good deal of shouting, whistling, and whooping before we found the place, and then we were not sure that it was not a nest of brigands. This was annoying, for I had converted a very large part of my worldly wealth into silver coin of the realm, and this was carried in canvas bags. I also had a few notes of the Bank of Persia, but there is no gold coinage, and the silver is in a debased currency and worth very little. However, all turned out well. We were taken to the house of the village elder, and shown into a beautifully carpeted room, entirely destitute of furniture ; we had to leave our boots outside, and squat on the ground. Our host, a stolid person with grave staring eyes, which he never kept off me, opened the ceremonial of reception by taking about half a dozen puffs at a very handsome silver pipe, which made a fearful row, and then we were fed. The food was brought in on enormous trays and placed on the floor before us. It consisted of various kinds of pillaus, curries, stewed chicken, kabob, or little bits of meat stuck on a skewer and roasted, and plenty of water. I drank brandy with

my water, and I made Churchill do the same. The
food was too rich and greasy to please my palate.
Later in the evening mattresses were brought in, and
beautiful embroidered coverlets, and I began to realise
that I was indeed in the East, and would have to
live on the floor and without furniture throughout this
expedition. That night we heard the jackals bark to
each other and reply, and knew that the next day
would be fine. We slept fairly well, and in the morning performed a hurried toilet, of a very perfunctory
nature. A large silver basin was brought in, a servant
held a silver ewer, and out of this he poured water
into our hands and over our faces. That was our
toilet, and for nearly a month that was all the washing
I had !

In a bright, clear, bracing morning we sallied forth
from the chieftain's hut and inspected the horses
provided for us. The scene had a somewhat martial
air, for a small party of the horsemen of the Ahmid
es Sultaneh was waiting for us. These were active,
workman-like looking little men on wiry mountain
ponies. They were armed with Martini-Henry carbines,
and wore a uniform resembling that of the Russian
Cossacks, except that they had the peculiar Tartar
fur cap, which looks like a huge mushroom.

The horse provided for me was a villainous beast
with a Roman nose and a sore on it.

This animal highly resented being mounted, and I
was very glad when I got rid of him. For the present

O

our road lay by the side of the Caspian, the blue sea to our right, the mountains and the jungle to our left. It was a beautiful and enjoyable ride, the pleasure of which was occasionally interrupted by the rivers which we had to ford, never an agreeable operation, but particularly unpleasant when one is mounted on an ill-tempered steed.

While we were thus riding along the shore of the Caspian, in brilliant weather, we espied in the distance a large cavalcade, which as we came nearer turned out to be headed by the brother and the son of the Ahmid es Sultaneh, and was composed of about fifty horsemen. After a due interchange of greetings we were now escorted to the mountain residence of my host at Kerganarud. The weather suddenly changed, and as we galloped through swamp and river the rain descended in torrents. One of the gallant escort lost his carbine in a river!

At Kerganarud we were made comfortable in the visitors' wing of the palace, and such a palace! It looked like a ruined prison, and was gorgeously furnished with tawdry, cheap Russian furniture and splendid Oriental carpets. The mixture of vulgarity and splendour was most incongruous. The brother of the Ahmid es Sultaneh was a jovial person, who bore a very strong personal resemblance to a popular and promising British naval officer of my acquaintance. I told him this, and he felt very flattered.

We were forcibly retained for nearly a week as the

guests of this Persian nobleman, for the rain was so
torrential that the country was partially flooded and
the rivers too swollen to cross. At length we started,
and I found that my Roman-nosed steed, full of beans
and vice, had not become more tractable for his rest.
We had not been many hours on our journey, during
which the troopers of our escort entertained us with
feats of horsemanship, when I had an unpleasant
adventure. But let me first say a few words about
these troopers. They were all short, light, active
men, without any fat about them, and apparently
made of leather and iron. As light cavalry they were
certainly preferable to the overgrown Cossacks of
Russia, who generally look too heavy for their little
ponies, but who, to my thinking, are better horsemen.
The horsemanship of the Persians is not remarkable.
Their saddles resemble those of the Cossacks, except
that they are larger and more like easy-chairs. They
ride with an absurdly short stirrup, and use a most
cruel bit, which has a plate of iron in the middle of
it. By pulling the bridle, this bit turns in the horse's
mouth, and the sharp end of the plate of iron is raised
to the palate, causing excruciating pain. The horse
prances and froths, and this is considered very pretty.
The Persian horseman keeps his horse's head well
up, and is continually tugging and worrying it. My
horse, probably accustomed to this sort of treatment,
and finding himself fitted with a mild European bit,
was very unmanageable.

. While we were racing each other on the grass, I had the greatest difficulty in keeping him from the jungle, from whence he could hear the seductive neighing of the wild mares. Finally he bolted with me and pelted into a bush, a projecting branch of which just missed my eye and sent me head over heels on the grass, greatly to the amusement of the escort. Of course the animal was caught and got a severe punishment, which made him behave himself.

At our next halting-place I was given a splendid mountain pony, as fine an animal as I could wish to ride, and very sorry I was when I had to part company with him later.

Never shall I forget that glorious ride along the shores of the Caspian. It was arranged in easy stages, never exceeding two menzils, or fifty miles a day, and sometimes not even as much as one menzil, that is about twenty-five miles. Followed by an escort of fifty mounted men, with young Churchill at my side to act as interpreter, and always attended by some local chieftain, or member of the Ahmid es Sultaneh's family, whose guest I either had been that night or was about to become, it was a most dignified progress, enlivened by pleasant and amusing incidents. Excruciatingly funny was the dear old brother of the Ahmid, who told me tales of his prowess against the Afghans, and how his brother and his men had fought against them and had "brought their fathers out of their graves," a splendid Persian expression which cannot be equalled even in the figurative American language.

Here and there on our journey, and dotted along the coast, we chanced upon small colonies of Russian fishermen, who came principally from the banks of the Volga, and were engaged in the caviarre trade. They looked like giants by comparison with the puny little Persians, broad-shouldered, blue-eyed, fair-haired, honest, simple, child-like and courteous, with a courtesy so different from that of the Oriental; they resembled the stalwart north-countrymen of home. They had brought their little Russia with them too. Their log-huts were Russian. In the corner of each room was the little ikon, which showed that each dwelling had been duly blessed by the priest, and they had their Russian bedding and black bread, everything complete. They were most hospitable, and gave us caviarre freshly prepared, and some of their delicious bread and salt to eat with it, and even some vodka!

I have travelled much in many parts of Russia, and in a good number of other countries besides, and I do not think that there is in the world a more charming, a more delightful, a more lovable creature than the average Russian peasant.

These Russians had little respect for the Persians, and we could see that the Persians feared and hated them. They live a hardy life on the desolate banks of the Caspian.

Here and there, too, we came upon Persian settlers who had returned as Russian subjects in the employment of Russian or Armenian merchants. These, who spoke Russian fluently, were loud in their praises of Russian institutions and freedom! and contrasted the benefits of Russian rule with the tyranny of Persia! All these things make one think.

At Astara my escort had dwindled down to two troopers, who came with me as far as Tabreez, and afterwards escorted young Churchill back to Resht. I had besides a graceless varlet called Yussuff, a servant of Mr. Churchill's, also lent me, who behaved in an exemplary manner while we were in the territory of the Ahmid es Sultaneh, but who now developed all the vices of the lazy servants of ancient romance, and, although a devout Mahomedan, who would not taste a morsel of food from sunrise to sunset during the great fast, he had no scruples about stealing my brandy. Astara is the frontier town of Persia; there are two Astaras side by side, one Russian and the port, the other Persian.

The Governor of Astara received us as all Orientals do, with great solemnity and a certain fierce savage hospitality, which makes one feel that they would kill one if they dared.

On the following morning we had to start by break of day, for we had a long and tedious journey before us. Between us and Ardabil, the next important town, there lay a steep and difficult mountain range,

which had to be ascended. When we had reached the
plateau beyond, we were to sleep in a village, and
then proceed to descend into the plain where stands
the ancient Persian capital of Ardabil.

In order to avoid entering Russian territory we had
to ford and re-ford a winding river something like
twelve times, but my splendid little pony was equal
to it, and behaved nobly. Presently we began the
ascent of the mountains, not, however, without having
had an occasional interchange of anything but compli-
ments with the Russian Cossack outposts, for it seems
that we were not always able to keep strictly within
Persian territory, the high road to Ardabil leading
to the Russian port of Astara, where the Caspian
steamers are in the habit of calling.

The ascent of that mountain range was grand,
perilous, and amazing. The little bridle-path which
skirted the precipice was frequently covered with
loose pebbles, along which the horses' hoofs slipped.
Occasionally we came upon loamy soil, into which the
horses sank up to their haunches. At other points
the road was skirted by rough rocks and so narrow
that we had to cock our legs up on the saddle to prevent their being ground against the rocks. Hundreds
of feet beneath us we could see mountain streams
gurgling and foaming in their courses. The sides of
the mountains were often beautifully wooded, and
altogether it was a most exciting ride, especially
when we met caravans of camels or little grey donkeys,

for which we had to make way by scrambling up the sides of the hills. The shouts of the drivers, the tinkling of the bells, the swearing of our own troopers, and the peril we were in, heightened the excitement of the situation. Truly quaint are these caravans, of which, in the course of my journey, I met great numbers. The camels are generally preceded by the queen camel, who wears a curious kind of bonnet or cap, quaintly decked out with ribbons, tassels, and bells. The dignity with which she carries these gaudy trappings, the daintiness with which she steps out on her gawky legs, and the ugly grace of her long neck, her protruding under-lip and her teeth, which remind one of the French caricatures of the English Mees of a bygone generation, makes one understand all the satire of the French name of *chameau* for an old maid.

Ardabil is a holy place; there are the shrines and tombs of the Shamuls, and the great Meshet, and so we were constantly coming across bands of pilgrims, and fakirs or hermits, on their return. These used to blow trumpets to announce their approach, and were quaintly dressed in white faced with red, and carrying strange staves surmounted by golden crescents. They always rode on white horses or asses, and usually sang doleful songs and begged for alms. Some of these fakirs were wild men, whose nakedness was scarcely covered, loathsome sights, who made hideous noises, and cursed us if we did not give them money.

At last, after many hours of toilsome travelling, we reached the snow-capped summit of the mountain. Here the air was cold and bracing, and the ground bare. A little shepherd boy made a great lamentation, telling us that one of his sheep had strayed and had been devoured by a wolf. We were all agog for the wolves; but, although we had a good look for them, we could not find any trace of the animals, though we saw the sheep huddled together in a cleft in the rocks, and trembling with fear. We now lost our way, and got among swampy ground. Darkness was upon us, and the village where we were to stop was not in sight. We had to dismount and walk gingerly by the sides of our horses, often sinking up to our knees in the swamp, until we got on to firm ground again. Our guide now recognised a landmark or two, and off we went at a hard gallop, and arrived at the village in the middle of the night. The dogs turned out and received us in true Oriental fashion, making a horrid noise. The intrepid Yussuff wasted a cartridge out of my revolver on one of them and killed it. All over the East the dogs are the scavengers, and Constantinople is not the only city where the pariah dogs are an eyesore, only they seem to be more tractable in the capital of the Sultan, and of a special breed.

Refreshed by a few hours' slumber, we rose early the next morning and started for Ardabil. The descent from the plateau in the early morning was a wonderful sight. We had left behind us the gorgeous vegetation which had charmed me at Resht, and which skirts the Caspian. Here were nothing but bare rocks and immense vistas of stony steppe. No trees, no habitations were in sight, and as we descended the plateau an illimitable expanse seemed to be unfolded before us. Hills and mountains looked like sugar-loaves. Colour was not wanting. Here tall peaks were covered with snow, others gilded by the rising sun, some looked red, some yellow, some purple. It was truly gorgeous ; but amidst all these mountains there lay straight in front of us a plain which seemed to extend for miles and miles, and was only bounded by the horizon. Through this plain there meandered, like a river, the track which had been followed for centuries, probably by successive caravans and travellers, while to the right and left of us the curious hills and mountains seemed to slope off and fade away into nothing. It was one of the most remarkable sights I have ever witnessed, and made a deep impression upon me.

At a sharp trot we now proceeded towards Ardabil. When at last that city came in sight, the trooper in charge of us begged us to wait while he proceeded to the city and gave notice of our approach.

What lies he told about us to the good people of Ardabil I am to this day in ignorance of, but I know that we had a royal reception. After about half an hour the trooper returned, and asked us to ride slowly.

At a short distance from the gates of the town a procession came to meet us. Preceded by an official, who
held a gaily caparisoned led-horse, and surrounded
by dignified Persians, I made my state entry into
Ardabil, and felt like the general of a conquering
army who is riding through a city which has capitu-
lated. The people all turned out and made obeisance
to me, and I had to bow to their salaams with due
dignity. We were taken, I verily believe, through
every street of that muddy city. The procession
lasted about half an hour. Then we came to the
Governor's palace, riding through gateways and
arches. I had to return the salutes of the sentries,
who presented arms as I passed; and what funny
soldiers they were! Arrived at the palace I dis-
mounted and walked through the courtyard, the
guard turning out. The Commandant of the palace,
a handsome young fellow, who seemed to feel that
this was an event in his life, received me with every
ceremony. He apologised for the absence of the
Governor, who was away, but introduced to me several
high functionaries, whose dignity and distinguished
bearing showed that they were men of importance.
After I had had some coffee and the inevitable Russian
cigarette—the Commandant and I were seated on
chairs, while a crowd of people, who came to pay me
court, had either to stand or to squat Oriental fashion
—we proceeded to the Meshed and saw the Mullahs
and Sayeds. On approaching this place of worship my

ears were saluted with the most horrible and uncanny
howling, like that of wild beasts.   In the courtyard, in
front of the Meshed, were some temporary tents or
huts, from whence this howling proceeded, and where
I could also hear the clank of chains.   I ascertained
that these places were tenanted by holy men who had
come there on a pilgrimage, and that they were
absolutely naked, and that the people came and gave
them alms and solicited their prayers and advice.   At
the door of the church there were crowds of sturdy
beggars.   The church itself was very interesting,
so were tombs of the Shamals, and the chambers
with the urns of the remains of their wives and
descendants ; but I was glad to get away.   On my
return the Commandant asked me how I liked the
place, and told me that all the Mullahs were scoundrels.   He had known an honest priest, but he
regretted to say that he was dead.   We were now
introduced to an Armenian, who had lived at Baku
and wore European clothes, and was, generally
speaking, a sort of worthy who had seen the world.
This individual had received *carte-blanche* to provide
us with a European dinner.   Ever since I had left
Resht I had been living on Persian foods—greasy
pillaus, kabobs, and other abominations, until I had
been seized with a sort of nausea for all kinds of
Oriental food.   The reader can imagine how delighted
I was to find myself seated at a table and on a
chair, and to have placed before me an excellent

and elaborate European dinner, which would have done credit to a Parisian restaurant, and which was washed down with excellent wines.

We were waited upon by a solemn individual, who also was our body-servant and assisted at my toilet, and who turned out to be the Mayor of Ardabil!

Our host, the smiling Commandant, refused to eat, but watched us with satisfaction. When our European dinner was over he asked us whether we would care to begin again, and now a Persian repast was served, which young Churchill walked into with a veracity that alarmed me.

At Ardabil I had to part with my good pony, which was sent back to the hills of Talish, and has since died, I hear. I engaged a man who provided horses for the journey to Tabreez, which now laid along the high road, and took us about a week. That journey was really hard. We slept in stables on the bare ground ; we fed on what we could shoot, and on eggs which had been boiled in oil, and had a horribly greasy flavour. On one occasion we came across a number of Armenians who wanted us to spend the night in their company, but our troopers warned us that they were brigands, and so we slept at another end of the village, with our guns and revolvers by our sides. When we once got into the high road we met crowds of people: women in litters, cara-vans of camels and donkeys, etc. Here and there we came upon the bodies of dead camels partially eaten by vultures. The camel will sometimes sit down and refuse to move. He is then relieved of his load and left to die. Donkeys have their peculiarities also. I have seen a donkey in sight of a town lie down in the mud, and refuse to stir, regardless of blows and objurgations, until his load was taken off, when he would merrily jump up and gallop into the khana, where he knew he was to spend the night.

On one occasion I saw a magnificent sight, a group of condors sitting on a rock, looking placidly into the vasty blue of the sky.

But throughout this journey I came upon no evidence of Persian vitality. A few interesting ruins here and there met the eye; but no new public buildings. The villagers were of a wretchedness beyond description. People live in mud huts, which have no value, and are frequently destroyed by a shower, only to be reconstructed the next day. The people have no furniture, no belongings, no property, no industries, no anything. I never saw a country in which the population seemed to be so abject. The carpet industry of Persia is completely ruined, and I was told at Ardabil, and later at Tabreez, that most of the Persian carpets are manufactured in England.

At length we arrived at the imposing town of Tabreez, which is approached by a fine avenue of trees, and is distinguished for its blue mosque and round towers.

As we approached the city we met an obvious Englishman in a pith helmet, and perfectly appointed with a native courier. This turned out to be the Tabreez agent of the British and Foreign Bible Society.

CHAPTER XI.

TABREEZ, like Resht, is a city of bazaars, but these
bazaars are more substantially built than at Resht,
and there is altogether a greater air of prosperity
than in the other city. The bazaars are nearly all
covered in and have a certain musty smell which
reminded me of the bazaars of Moscow. There are
no European hotels at Tabreez and so we made
straight for the house of the English Consul-General,
a handsome building standing in its own grounds and
guarded by a strong body of porters, mostly colonels
in the Persian artillery, from which class the porters
of the various consulates are apparently principally
recruited. The Russian Consul, I afterwards learned,
was able to live in much greater state, possessed an
escort of about one hundred Cossacks, and was a man
of influence and power. But Mr. Godfrey Wood, our
Consul-General, who has spent all his life in the East
and is well acquainted with the Oriental mind, has
made a bold fight, and stands up to his Russian
colleague with admirable pluck. He has organised

a racing club among the European colony, among
which there are several English merchants, and a
small staff of clerks, attached to the Imperial Bank,
besides the telegraph people, and of course the Bible
Society officials and missionaries, who are naturally
not given to sport.

Riding through Tabreez one is at once struck by
the fact that here is a different race of people, more
sturdy and vigorous than those which inhabit the
Caspian littoral. They have, indeed, very little pure
Persian blood in them and are of Tartar origin,
racially akin to the Afghans I believe, and even
speak a language entirely different from that spoken
in the south.

Mr. Wood had gone out for his daily drive when
we arrived. This daily drive we afterwards ascertained
was a very important ceremonial function. Preceded
by out-riders in uniform, and surrounded by a small
cavalcade, Mr. Wood took the air in a handsome
victoria drawn by two spirited and well-appointed
horses. People saluted him in the streets as he
passed. This ceremony was necessary, because the
Russian Consul, with his mounted Cossacks, cut an
imposing figure, except that his equipage was not
nearly so well appointed or so smart as Mr. Wood's,
and this the Persians appreciated.

As Mr. Wood was out we consulted—travel-stained
and weary, we had not had a bath or even a decent
wash for something like three weeks—on what we

should do, when Mr. Wood's housekeeper appeared, took upon herself to ask us in, and, looking at me critically, asked me whether I should like to have a bath. Here, I thought, is true hospitality! In about an hour I had made myself fairly clean and presentable, and was able to saunter into Mr. Wood's drawing-room with the air of a man who was calling on his friend in Mayfair. Oh! the luxury of being clean! And the luxury of being again in a well-appointed English house, with good food and good wines, and even whiskey! Mr. Wood was kindness itself. We had arrived at a most inconvenient time. His wife and family were down with diphtheria or scarlatina, or some such awful complaint. It turned out to be a false alarm, and we were very soon introduced to the rest of his household. For that day at least it was a man's party, and very jolly it was after dinner to sit in a comfortable arm-chair, smoking a pipe, sipping our whiskey, and talking over things in general.

"Do you know what these are made of?" Mr. Wood asked me, as he handed me an ash-tray of papier-mâché.

"They look like papier-mâché," I replied.

"So they are," he said; "but they are made of British Bibles. You have no idea what a boon these Bibles are to the village industries of Persia."

I was very much amused at this statement, and naturally accepted it with the proverbial grain of salt;

but I have since ascertained that Mr. Wood's information was absolutely trustworthy. Indeed, our missionary efforts in Mahomedan countries can scarcely
be described as altogether successful. A predecessor
of Mr. Wood's had turned the consulate into a sort of
chapel, and had held regular Salvationist meetings in
it ; but I am afraid that the solid benefits which he thus
conferred on the community were few, and the spiritual
good doubtful. It is sad to think that the cause of
Christianity frequently suffers through the over
zealous and often injudicious action of people who,
however estimable they are in many respects, are
lamentably deficient in a sense of humour. Christianity has made but little progress in Mahomedan
countries, and I cannot help thinking that this is
largely due to the fact that the methods adopted for
spreading it are too distinctively European to meet with
response in Oriental minds. Still the missionaries are
doing excellent work, although they seem to have
more success with the Armenians, who are Christians
already, than with the Mahomedans. On the Turkish
frontier, near the shores of Lake Urumiyah, and in
the neighbourhood of Khoi, the missionaries carry
their lives in their hands. This district is rendered
most unsafe by bands of Kurdish brigands, who
acknowledge no authority and are a constant source
of danger. As for the district in Kurdistan itself
between Van and Khoi, I was told it was absolutely
dangerous at present. The Kurds were in open revolt,

the caravans were being attacked, and generally a state of anarchy existed. Mr. Wood had despatched his vice-Consul, with an escort, to Khoi and Urumiyah to report upon the condition of things, and was anxiously awaiting his return when we arrived.

On the following morning I called on the Armenians who had been indicated to me at Tiflis, and was surprised to find how distance seems to distort the mental vision. These Armenians, who had been represented to me as bold, daring, and faithful, who would take me across the frontier, and who were obliged to do so by the conditions of their membership of some secret society or other, proved to be very lukewarm in their offers of assistance. They confirmed what I had heard from Mr. Wood, namely, that the regions of the frontier were in a state of anarchy, and that the Turkish Government had issued strict instructions prohibiting people from entering or leaving Turkey by way of Persia.

"We could smuggle you across," they said; "but we cannot guarantee your getting to Van. The Kurdish brigands will murder you, and nobody will know what has become of you. The same fate befell Lenz, the American cyclist, who was making a tour round the world—it has befallen, very probably, Mr. Fitzgerald, of the *Daily News*. What possible object would be served by your losing your life in such a useless enterprise? You will obtain no information that you have not already obtained at Tiflis.

You do not speak the language. What do you propose to do? Even supposing you get safely to Van, your troubles would then only begin. It is true that there are means of concealing you at Van; but how you are to be conveyed from Van to Bitlis or Moosh, both garrison towns and full of Turkish soldiers, we do not see. Besides, it is quite unnecessary for the Turks to arrest you. The Kurdish brigands can put you out of the way without causing the Turkish authorities any trouble. This will probably happen after you have passed Khoi, for you may be quite sure that the Turkish authorities have got their eye on you."

Of this I was speedily to have a convincing proof. I had not returned to the consulate long before a gentleman with an Armenian name was announced. He spoke French, told me that he had been the Persian Commissioner to the Chicago World's Fair, that he knew I was an English journalist, and was ready to offer me his services to smuggle me across the frontier. I told him that I was no journalist, but an English tourist, that I had had no intention of going across Turkey, but that if he really thought he could get me through that way I should be inclined to consider his offer, as anything in the shape of an adventure was an attraction to an Englishman. I then asked him to call again the following day with particulars of his proposal, and I would think over his idea in the meantime.

He had not been gone long before I ascertained from a trustworthy source that he was in the service of the Turkish Government, and had really been sent over by the Turkish Consul to see what I was like.

That evening Mr. Wood told me that the Turkish Consul was making inquiries about me, and that I had better go and see him and get my passport viséed for Trebizond.

This I boldly did, the Turkish Consul receiving me with great courtesy. He told me, however, that he had instructions not to *visé* the passports of journalists, as His Majesty the Sultan did not wish journalists to travel through the disturbed districts of Kurdistan.

"If you are simply a tourist, as you say," he continued, " I would strongly advise not to risk your life in crossing over the Persian frontier into Turkey. The roads are very unsafe, Kurdish and Armenian brigands abound, and if you should get murdered you will only have yourself to blame. Disturbances have occurred in this neighbourhood, and hence, if you insist on taking this route you must clearly understand that you are doing so at your own risk ; the Government cannot be expected to be responsible for you. Of course, if nothing will deter you from going this way I shall *visé* your passport ; but I must warn you that that will be of very little avail."

This was certainly what is called " the straight tip " in sporting parlance.

Mr. Wood himself did not do anything to weaken

the effect of the Turkish Consul's words. He told me that he knew I was being watched, and that he felt pretty certain that I should be murdered.

"In fact," he added, "so strongly do I feel on this subject that I would, if I had the power, cause you to be arrested in order to prevent you from going across, and thus save your life."

He urged upon me in the strongest words to at least write home for instructions before undertaking this foolhardy expedition, as he called it. I followed his advice the more readily as my funds were running low, and besides, completely cut off as I was from news and European papers, I could not tell whether the public interest in the Armenian question was still as keen as ever. I sent my telegram over the English wires and got a reply brief and peremptory : " Return." I naturally concluded that the Armenian question had once more "fizzled out," and prepared to leave *viâ* Julfa and Erivan, the very route which the Governor-General of the Caucasus had especially prohibited my taking. There was an element of danger in this which recompensed me for being compelled to give up my original plan ; besides, there was a chance of my being able to visit Etchmiadzin, and that I felt would be much more interesting than visiting the scenes of the Sassun massacres, where there was nothing left for me to see, and whither the European Commission was believed to be already travelling. Mr. Wood very kindly sent my passport over to the Russian consulate, where it was viséed for Europe *via* Russia, and I commenced making preparations for my departure.

Having parted with young Churchill and the scapegrace Yussuff, I now had to engage a servant and make arrangements to go " chuppa," or at a gallop, literally, which is the usual method of posting on the high roads of Persia. Just as I had got everything ready for my journey, a fresh downpour set in, and I was prevailed upon, not with great difficulty, to remain a few more days in the comfortable house of the English Consul-General until the rain should have subsided.

I thus had leisure to study a little the situation at Tabreez. Tabreez is within a three days' journey of the Russian frontier; but here Russian influence does not make itself so conspicuously felt as at Resht. There is also a very large Armenian population, which cannot be described as being particularly favourably disposed to Russia. Here, as everywhere else where Armenians occur in these Eastern countries, Russia not excepted, they are the centres of culture and education. The Armenian schools of Tabreez are excellent, and compare favourably with those of Tiflis. Devoted Armenian men and women, highly cultured, and educated in some European country, are giving their lives to the noble task of teaching and bringing up the rising generation of Persian Armenians. They receive in

return a bare pittance, upon which they are just able
to support a penurious life. They are all plain livers
and high thinkers. Round Urumiyah there are
Armenian settlements and American and English
missionaries, who are doing excellent work. Tabreez
is the seat of the Patriarch of the Persian Armenians,
who is under the jurisdiction, like the Patriarch of
Constantinople, of the Catholicos at Etchmiadzin.
These Armenians, cut up between Turkey, Russia,
and Persia, are really one nation, recognise one head,
and are longing for some form of national unity.

Tabreez is really the northern capital of Persia,
it is in a line with Cyprus, and on the high road
to Teheran. Russia would therefore like to see
General Kourapatkin's strategic railway rapidly completed. Why England should not build a counter-
railway is one of those conundrums which the high
priests of diplomacy would probably answer very
wisely.

For my part, I think that a railway from Alexandretta, *viâ* Diarbekir, Bitlis, Van, and Tabreez, would
be an excellent idea, and would materially help
Russia in achieving her great civilising mission in
Asia Minor, and enable us perhaps to stop her from
carrying that mission too far.

There can be no doubt that Tabreez is a centre of
intrigue, a sort of caldron where many currents meet
and bubble. The Armenians, as I have said, are
numerous ; but there is, unfortunately, little solidarity

among them, for there are spies and traitors in their midst. On the frontier, however, the Armenians, according to all accounts, are more sure of themselves, and even able to present a bold front to the Kurdish brigands who infest the neighbourhood. One thing at all events is certain, and that is that under Persian rule the Armenians enjoy relatively more freedom than under Turkey or even Russia. They are, as I cannot too often repeat, the soul of Persian commerce. During my journey there I frequently came upon bands of Armenian commercial travellers going to Astara, and, as we have seen, at Ardabil for instance, Armenians enjoy the favour of the ruling Powers.

Provided with a Persian servant who spoke a little Russian, I now proceeded to Julfa, the Russian frontier town, which is about three days' journey. We went chuppa—that is galloping all the way—and a most enjoyable ride it was. At distances of about twenty-five miles apart I changed horses at the little post-stations, at some of which I had to spend the night, where I had to sleep on the bare ground, for European beds are unknown, and the Scriptural injunction to the sick man by Our Lord "to take up his bed and walk" is not so difficult to accomplish as we Europeans imagine. Indeed, a journey through the East helps to make us understand the Scriptures more clearly. The house-tops are flat, and generally used as we do courtyards, gardens, and balconies—for purposes of taking the air. The houses are so flimsily built that we can well understand how important it is that they should be erected upon rocks. Frequently when the rains descend and beat upon the houses of Tabreez entire neighbourhoods are destroyed and washed away.

I arrived at Julfa on the Easter Saturday of 1895, slept like a top in the Oriental hostelry, which is maintained on the Persian side of the river which divides Persia from Russia. My couch was composed of mattresses and coverlets placed on the floor ; there were, indeed, one or two wooden beds, but, having a wholesome dread of insects, I preferred to sleep on the floor.

The communication between Russia and Persia at Julfa is kept up by a ferry-boat, which resembles nothing so much as an enormous packing-case. The next morning being Easter Sunday, this boat would not run, and so I had the pleasure of spending the whole day indoors, for it was pelting with rain outside, and looking over into Russian territory, where I could occasionally distinguish a Cossack belonging to the Frontier police walking across a large square. The Persian Julfa is built of mud ; that of Russia of wood. There is an ugly Russian wooden church in the centre of this frontier town the domes and cupolas of which are painted a bright green, as is the abiding custom of the Russians.

On Easter Monday, in a drizzling rain, I was at last able to get taken over. Of all my experiences, that was perhaps the most unpleasant that I ever went through. I was jambed into this packing-case of a ferry-boat, which was flat-bottomed and had four perpendicular sides, but no seats. It was about fifty feet long by ten broad, and was filled to overflowing by a quantity of Persian emigrants, navvies, and work-people, all indescribably filthy, infested with vermin, and all yelling at the tops of their voices. Among the passengers was a horse, which was got in with great difficulty, but got out more easily. The River Aras is a turbulent swift-flowing stream, which was much swollen by recent floods, and things did not look at all hopeful; still, we managed to get across, and then I had to carry my luggage for about a mile to the custom-house, for I had dismissed my servant, who could now be of no use to me, but might, on the contrary, cause me trouble.

Some time was spent in finding the custom-house officials, for Easter Monday is quite as great a holiday in Russia as it is in England; but when these were once found I was treated with the same polite-ness and courteousness which I have ever experienced from the officials of the Tzar. My passport was in order, my gun was winked at, and I was allowed to proceed. My next care was to engage a conveyance at the post-house, and here I discovered that the only means of progress was an open springless cart, drawn by two horses. This was pleasant in a drizzling rain; but I had my Persian abbah of camel's hair, and this did me good service, for it turned out to be absolutely watertight.

It was now getting late, and since early morning I had not had a morsel of food, but anything like a meal was out of the question. There is no inn at Julfa. In a miserable sort of grocer's shop, kept by an atrocious Jew, I bought some bread and half a smoked sausage. This I eat, while I washed it down with some coarse vodka. Then I leapt into the springless cart, and presently, in the face of a pitiless drizzle, I was bumped along at a fearful rate over an unmacadamised track, composed principally of ruts. The springless cart shook every bone of my body, till I thought I could hear my vertebræ rattle in my back, and occasionally I was in imminent peril of being pitched out. I drove through a waste and wild track of country, with little to recommend it. Here and there I started some cock, but as my gun was not loaded, and I did not feel in a very sporting humour, I did not try to shoot anything. Occasionally I met doubtful characters on the road, who eyed my gun respectfully, but even these were rare. At long intervals I came upon police-stations which have been established by the Government to keep the road free from brigands. In this the police have not been very successful, for they are recruited from the very tribes who supply the robbers. Villainous faces these Cossacks have, and I am informed that they are mostly in collusion with their tribesmen, the brigands. But Russia is a poor country, and has large tracts of barren land on her hands, and so she has to do the best she can.

That night I slept on a hard wooden bench in a vile and filthy post-house. On the whole I cannot recommend my method of spending the Easter Monday of 1895 as either enjoyable or invigorating.

It took three days' open-cart driving—such a cart is called a "tarantass"—before I reached Erivan, and, notwithstanding its many discomforts, it was an interesting, though bone-shaking, drive. Of course the food at the wayside inns consisted principally of sausage and black bread. It was not until I reached Erivan that I was able to taste any cooked food.

Gradually, as I got farther away from the Persian frontier, the country began to improve in appearance, and villages came in sight. As I drove into these villages I noticed a board on a sign-post on which was written in Russian the name of the village, the population, and the creed of the people. Thus I was able to distinguish, as the population grew more dense, between Mussulman, Armenian, and Russian villages. Very soon, however, I found that it was quite unnecessary to look at these boards. After passing several of these villages I was able to distinguish the race they belonged to without any such assistance. The condition of the Armenian peasantry reminded me of that of the peasantry of Poland, and is infinitely superior to that of the typical Russian peasant of

Central Russia or even the Volga. The fields were all well cultivated, the cows were well fed, the horses well groomed. The various carts and agricultural implements I saw in the Armenian villages were far superior to anything one sees in Russia. The men were all tall and handsome, and very intelligent-looking fellows, neat in their dress, and very proud and haughty in their bearing. The women were modest and seemed to avoid the gaze of strangers. In these Armenian villages the roads were good, the houses clean and well built. In short, the contrast between them and the Mussulman villages was apparent at a long distance. And yet people have reproached the Armenians with being a non-agricultural race !

Of the Russian villages and settlements of dissenters I shall have a few words to say later.

In the inn in which I spent my second night I was the witness of a curious scene. On my arrival the passage was full of drunken Cossacks, at whose head was an equally drunken officer. What was remarkable was that this officer was a puny, wizen, miserable specimen of humanity, about five foot nothing, while his men were all splendid fellows, some of them six foot three in their boots, but hopelessly brutalised, and evidently fearing neither God nor devil ; but their obedience to, and affection for, their little officer was amusing to witness. This was a loud-voiced, insolent little beast, who was bent on persecuting an unfortunate post official who had been sent down on a tour of inspection, and was evidently on his way to some neighbouring post town. He had locked himself in his room, and was pleading from behind his door, in a plaintive voice, to be left alone and allowed to go to sleep, as he had to get up early. But the officer kept hammering at his door, and threatened to drive it in if the post-office official did not come out and stand treat all round. At last the door was opened, and a pale, emaciated figure in the uniform of the Russian post-office showed itself. Immediately the officer called to his men, and shouted, "Now then, children, seize him!"

Before the unoffending civilian knew where he was, he was seized by the Cossacks, thrown up to the ceiling and caught again, this tossing being continued amidst shouts and military cheers. "We won't let you go till you stand treat! This is holiday time," the officer shouted. The official's face was a study. He was evidently in terror of his life, and looked as white as a sheet; but he remained obdurate, protesting that he had no money. At last the Cossacks got weary of their prey. "Well, this is no use," said the little officer; "we must go somewhere else and see whether we cannot get a drink from another quarter"; and they departed. With such intellectual amusements do the weary officers in these distant stations while away the time. I am told that at some places they play at being the members of a farmyard, each player having to take the part of some fowl or animal, and imitate its voice.

While I was watching the riotous conduct of these gallant defenders of the Russian Empire, a mysterious individual, with police-spy written on every line of his countenance, accosted me, and asked who I was and whither I was going. I promptly told him this was no business of his, and retired into my room.

At another inn the attendant asked me whether I could intercede for him with the Emperor. It appeared that he was a dissenter from the neighbourhood of Kieff. He had joined an evangelical sect somewhat resembling that started by Count Tolstoy. This was his only crime, and for it he had been exiled to this distant region for life. He did not know what had happened to his wife and children, whether they were alive or dead, or in want.

On my journey through the Caucasus I came across entire settlements of Molokane, another sect of dissenters, who had been exiled for their religion. Their villages looked like those of the Dutch, owing to the remarkable cleanliness of their cottages. The women are beautiful, and the men industrious. Frequently I met large carts or vans laden with these Molokane, who were on their way to the region to which they had been exiled.

While this kind of religious persecution, to say nothing of the outrages on the Jews, is common in Russia, there are yet people in England, who read the papers, simple enough to believe that Russia will befriend the persecuted Armenians of Turkey!

Q

CHAPTER XII.

ETCHMIADZIN.

It was a fine bright morning when I arrived at Erivan, one of the oldest of Armenian cities, and was deposited at the post-house. Erivan is the capital of a Russian province, has a Governor-General, and is provided with all the bureaucratic machinery of what is called a "Government" town. It was the first town of importance that I had struck since leaving Tabreez. I had ascertained that Etchmiadzin was within easy distance of Erivan, and that I could possibly manage to pay that monastery a visit without exciting attention. I had also learned that there was a diligence service from Erivan to the nearest point on the Trans-Caucasian Railway, and I thought it would be a good plan to take this diligence, as I would probably attract less notice if I travelled with a number of other people than if I posted it in solitary grandeur.

At the post-house I was informed by a bright-eyed intelligent Armenian that the diligence would not start until the following day.

" Dear me ! " I said, dolefully. " What am I to do with myself in this miserable place for twenty-four hours ? "

"Oh ! " said the intelligent Armenian, " you could pay a visit to the monastery of Etchmiadzin. It is well worth seeing."

" Etchmiadzin ? " I said. " Where is that ? I have never heard of the place before."

"Oh ! it is a ten mile drive from here and would repay a visit."

" So be it then. I will go to Etchmiadzin. Order me a carriage. But first tell me where the baths are, for I must have a bath."

In Persia the public baths are filthy. The water in the pool or plunge is not changed from week's end to week's end, and I had often seen on my journey the naked figures of Persian men running out to cool themselves after their bath, and looking indescribably dirty. Horrid gaunt, lanky figures they were. But the Russian baths, especially in a Government town, are generally luxurious, and I felt I should be comparatively safe in trusting myself to one. Nevertheless, this was a great tactical error. If I had not had this fatal craze for cleanliness I might have slipped through the Caucasus without detection, but this was not to be.

I proceeded along the street in the direction indicated by the Armenian innkeeper, towards the baths, when I suddenly came upon a higher police functionary attended by a policeman. He shouted to me to stop, and beckoned to me to cross the road and give an account of myself.

"Who are you?" he said; "how long have you been here? where do you come from?" he asked, in one breath.

I saluted him politely, and told him I was a British subject travelling from Tabreez and on my way to London, in confirmation of which statement I produced my passport, and showed him that it had been viséed for Europe *via* the Caucasus.

" When did you arrive ? "

" This morning, and I am just on my way to the baths, for I am very dirty. Could you tell me whether I am in the right direction for the bath ? "

" Yes," he replied; "go straight on, and turn to the right. On your way you will pass the police station. Will you be so good as to leave your passport there. I am the chief of police here and have strict instructions to *visé* the passports of all travellers."

" Certainly," I said, quite unconcernedly, but feeling inwardly that I was in a regular fix.

" That is the man I told you about, and reported to your Excellency," said the policeman.

" I beg your pardon," I answered, " but I do not think you could have seen me before, seeing that I have only just arrived at Erivan."

The chief of police, who was a very gentlemanly person, repeated his request that I should report myself, and then went on. There was nothing for it, so I traced my steps to the police station, which I easily recognised by the conning tower of the fire-brigade, and left my passport with an official who looked as though he was preserved in vodka.

Thereupon I had my bath and returned to the post-house, when I told my Armenian friend my experience with the police.

"That is all right, sir," he said. "I will see that you get your passport by to-morrow morning."

"Look here!" I replied, "I do not mind paying for it, but I must have my passport in order by to-morrow morning, so as to be able to start by the diligence."

"I will look after that," the Armenian said. "If you are now going to Etchmiadzin ask for Z——. He is a very educated monk and a very nice man, and he will show you over the place."

A wink is often as good as a nod, and so I acted on my new found friend's suggestion.

Seated in a capital victoria, the springs of which made me feel myself in Paradise after my experience of the hard unyielding tarantass, drawn by a pair of capital horses, I was whirled at a pleasant pace to the capital of Armenian religious life.

All along the road—as indeed I had been for the last twenty-four hours—I was haunted by Mount Ararat, which stood immovable in the distance, and from which there seemed to be no getting away. The monastery and religious town of Etchmiadzin, with its seminary and cathedral, whose quaint sugar-loafed steeples look so funny, has in front of it a suburb in which are the residences of the Russian officials, and the few other lay individuals, shopkeepers, etc., who have clustered round this centre.

As I drove through the broad street of this suburb, I saw a stout Russian officer sitting on the balcony of a house, in front of which were posted a couple of police sentinels. A mounted policeman was talking to him.

He did not at first see us; and it was not until I had passed that I heard him shouting to the driver to know who I was. The mounted policeman had by this time galloped off towards Erivan. The officer, my driver told me, was the Police Prefect of Etchmiadzin, and I had had a narrow escape of being turned back.

Arrived at the seminary, or ecclesiastical college of Etchmiadzin, I had some difficulty in finding the worthy monk to whom I had been recommended, and whom I will not do the bad service of further particularising. He received me with the greatest cordiality, and I thought the wisest course for me to adopt was to tell him frankly and fully who I was.

He told me that the attitude of the Russian Government towards the Armenians had within recent years undergone a great change, and that Russia was in her way, and by more civilised methods, doing just as much to exterminate the Armenian race as Turkey.

"The great difficulty we Armenians have to-day is to get education," he said. "We are an ancient race with a noble literature and a great cultural history behind us, but everything is being done to undermine that culture, to reduce us to the condition of brutes, to make us learn Russian, forget and neglect our own language, and thus become assimilated by Russia. But the Russians are intellectually, culturally, and racially our inferiors, and we mean to do all we can to retain our superiority."

The eyes of the haughty monk flashed, his pure and almost girlishly modest face flushed crimson, and I felt that a patriot was standing before me.

"In our seminary and schools we have a number of scholars from all parts of Armenia, Persia, Turkey, and Russia, and we do what we can to make them intelligent and high-spirited. The most stupid boys are those who come from the Turkish towns. Some of those who have been educated by missionaries are bright lads. Formerly we enjoyed the rights of sanctuary, but latterly this has been taken away from us. Immediately after the Sassun massacres, large numbers of refugees came over, and we were able to feed and clothe and help a large number of them; although quite recently the Russian Government has taken our right of sanctuary from us; we are not permitted to give shelter to people without passports, and I may just as well tell you that we are practically under police surveillance. But come, let me show you the sights."

This kindly monk now took me round and showed me the remarkable Cathedral of Etchmiadzin, which it is said was built some eight hundred years ago by a pious hermit, to whom the injunction to build this cathedral on this particular site had been communicated in a dream, in which also the shape and architectural features, dimensions, and interior arrangements had been likewise revealed. Thus this cathedral came to be the model upon which all Armenian churches have been built. It contains a miraculous picture of the Virgin, about which there is quite a literature of legendary lore. The altar stands in the centre. In this cathedral is kept the sacerdotal oil with which every true Armenian, wheresoever he may be, must be anointed on the occasion of his birth and marriage, and before his death. The oil, which is blessed by the Catholicos, who is the head of the Church, is distributed from time to time to every part of the world where there is an Armenian Church.

From the cathedral, where I examined the gorgeous vestments and many curious relics, I was taken to the celebrated tank in the garden of the monastery where are kept the famous Armenian fish.

I was then handed over to another monk, who spoke German—in which language we conversed—and taken to see the library.

This monk, an archdeacon I believe he was, had been educated in Berlin, and had been originally intended for the Church. He had embraced the religious life from a passionate love for his race, and as the Armenian religion is to-day practically the only remaining symbol of Armenian national unity, he has devoted his life to it. He was, like all the monks I saw at Etchmiadzin, an extremely refined, cultured, and well-educated man. High thinking and plain living seemed to be the motto of these simple, gentle, courteous Armenian ecclesiastics. I have seen the monks of Kieff, Moscow, and St. Petersburg, but these cannot compare for a moment with the lofty and noble Armenians.

The library of Etchmiadzin is world-famed. Here was recently discovered, by an English scholar, a celebrated gospel, more than a thousand years old, magnificently bound in a beautiful Ravenna binding. There are something like three thousand illuminated manuscripts in this literary treasure-house.

While I was looking over the interesting manuscripts, testaments, bindings, portraits, and other remarkable objects, a gentleman came up to us and said to my *cicerone*, in German :

"You speak German. You seem to be a well-educated man for an Armenian monk ? "

The monk smiled, but did not make any reply.

"Have you come across an English officer, a Colonel Clark, who is travelling over the Caucasus, looking into this Armenian question?" the Russian continued, darting a suspicious and penetrating look at me. I am afraid my appearance was calculated to excite suspicion. I was attired in a loose brown abbah, a cloak of camel's hair, under which I had a reefer jacket, knickerbockers, and heavy Russian riding-boots, reaching above the knee. I wore besides a grey felt wide-awake hat, and a Persian walking stick. A beard of six weeks' growth or more adorned my countenance, and the hair of my head was cropped short like that of a convict.

The monk replied to the inquisitive querist that he did not know anything of Colonel Clark.

"And who are you?" asked the Russian, turning on me severely; "you seem to speak German also."

I told him that I did not think it was his business; but he replied that he was the civilian official of the Governor-General, and that it was his business. So I told him, what was absolutely true, that I was born in Berlin, that I had been in Persia on business, and coming back found that I had to wait a day at Erivan for the diligence. Erivan seemed a dull, stupid place, and I had not known what to do with myself, so my innkeeper had advised me to look at this strange old monastery.

"Yes," said the official, with a sneer, "Erivan is a dull place. Where is your passport?"

"At the Erivan police-office," I replied promptly.

"Well," said the official, turning to the monk, "I

suppose they will make a bishop of you soon ; with your knowledge of German and foreign languages, I dare say you are very useful."

With these words he left us, and I was taken to the palace of the Catholicos, which was certainly simplicity itself. Very few signs of luxury could I discover. The Catholicos himself was away, I had seen him at Tiflis and had been entrusted by him with a mission to the English people, which was duly published in the *Daily Graphic* for February 26th, 1895, and I may here quote the passage in which it occurs :—

"On my arrival at Tiflis it was my good fortune to find the Catholicos had not yet left, as had been reported, that he was still lingering on, but that his ultimate destination was shrouded in mystery. He was living at the Armenian Episcopal Palace at Tiflis, where he was besieged all day long by visitors of all sorts and conditions; for he is, it must be remembered, apart from his position as head of the Church, perhaps the most popular man in Armenia. He is seventy-five years of age, but, notwithstanding his years, still prefers riding on horse-back to every other form of travelling. He is, I am told, a capital shot, and has, so it is whispered, more than once shot his man—in self-defence, of course. His seat is at Etchmiadzin, almost on the frontier of Turkey, and he probably knows more about what is actually going on at Sassun than anybody who does not live there. He is considered a great orator and also a great author. Besides this he is a holy man of great austerity and deep piety, though genial and kindly. Such a man, it is needless to say, is well calculated to fill the popular imagination.

"The palace of the bishops of Tiflis is not very palatial in appearance. It is a plain white building with two stories, standing in a courtyard, the toy-shop cathedral fronting it.

"After applying for an audience I was received by the Catholicos in a very plain sort of drawing-room, the walls of which were bare. The furniture consisted of a sofa, a table, and a few chairs. The Catholicos, who was somewhat indisposed, occupied the sofa. He is a man of imposing presence, over six feet three in height, with fire in his eye, and a majestic simplicity of demeanour. His white flowing beard has still many streaks of gold. He has the nose of a warrior, and the mouth of an orator. Owing to my ignorance of Armenian, the editor of the Armenian *Echo* acted very kindly as my interpreter. His Holiness was attired in an ample fox-skin fur coat, and wore on his head a purple velvet cap, somewhat similar to the head-coverings worn by the Greek priests.

"The Catholicos received me with frank cordiality, grasped my hand instead of stretching forth his own to be kissed, and shook it heartily. Although, as I have said before, I was unable to understand him, there was a peculiar fascination in listening to the musical cadence of his voice and the sonorous phrases which it uttered. Of course, in the peculiar circumstances of his case, it was extremely difficult for him to allow himself to be 'drawn,' but from his answers to a few questions I put, I understood the following. His attitude is one of strict legality. Before being the Catholicos of Armenia, he is above all things the loyal subject of the Emperor of Russia, and must in everything submit himself to the authority of his sovereign. Therefore the Catholicos does not wish it to be thought that he had determined upon any individual line of action with regard to the oppressed sheep of his flock. These were immediately under the care of the Patriarch of Constantinople, with whom he stood in direct relations. When I told him that in Trebizond there was a belief that he intended to visit the disturbed districts, he smiled and looked extremely pleased; but our intermediary conveyed to me that as the Patriarch had difficulty in obtaining permission for a delegate of his own to visit the places in question, it was not probable that he would be allowed to do so, even supposing he had that intention. I then asked him whether he wished to send any message through me to the English people, and he charged me to convey them his benediction. He bestowed his benediction on the Queen, who was always the friend of the poor and oppressed, and also on that great and noble people whose instincts were ever on the side of freedom, and who had together done so much for Armenia."

In a subsequent letter I described the departure of the Catholicos from Tiflis to Batoum. He was attired in his majestic black robes and hood, and was attended by body-guards in scarlet and gold, and followed by a long train of bishops and clergy. He drove through the streets of Tiflis in

"a closed carriage with four horses and an outrider, and with two scarlet body-guards mounted behind. The carriage was preceded by two venerable priests with flowing white beards, mounted on grey horses and carrying banners, one the standard of the Catholicos, the other the standard of the Bishop of Tiflis. A long line of carriages brought up the rear, and the whole procession was escorted by mounted Cossacks. The concourse of people was tremendous, and vociferous cheering rent the air as the aged prelate drove to the station, where a special train awaited him. A friend who accompanied him, and has just returned, tells me that the railway was lined all the way with people, and that the train had frequently to slow down, so as to avoid running over the enthusiastic throng. At one of the stations a splendid banquet was served, and the soldiers of an Armenian regiment which is stationed there turned out to receive the Catholicos. His ultimate destination is still a secret. But no monarch could travel with greater pomp or receive a heartier ovation."

The Catholicos is the Pope of the Armenian Church, has the title of Holiness, and is elected by the suffrages of the entire Armenian community. He is at once the spiritual head of an ancient and respectable religion and the personification of the national unity of the Armenians. As such, he is therefore an extremely interesting and important national figure. He is a much travelled man, who has visited the capitals of Europe, and whose fearless eloquence on behalf of the community which he represents, obtained for him his election. My visit to his private residence convinced me of the truth of Gibbon's statement that the austerity of the lives of the Armenian prelates increases in just proportion to the elevation of their rank. But the austerity and simplicity of the Catholicos has added little to the esteem in which he is held. On the other hand, his strictly loyal attitude towards Russia has been attributed to cowardice rather than to wisdom. The laity of Armenia are profoundly disappointed in him, nor the laity only. The feeling of disillusionment and discontent has spread to the more enlightened and active of the clergy.

The Armenian clergy may be conveniently divided

into two categories : the simple, ignorant, but pious and obedient ecclesiastics of the old school, whose minds are but little occupied with questions outside the domain of religion and ritual ; and the younger, intelligent, and often highly educated priests, who look upon their religion more as a political institution than a creed, and dream of reuniting the scattered members of the Armenian race in one grand Armenian nation. These have but scant regard for the old superstitions with which the Armenian religion has become incrustated. They are mostly enlightened and broad-minded, and many of them have little vocation for a religious life, having, in the majority of cases, embraced it purely as a convenient cloak for political propaganda. Some of them have told me that they now regretted entering the Church, the discipline of which considerably hampered their activity, and others even went so far as to say that they were disgusted with the supineness of the more exalted members of the hierarchy, and that if they had known how little vigour the Catholicos would display in the present national emergency, they would not have voted for him, and would in fact never have taken orders.

These political monks and priests are nevertheless a great source of strength to the present national movement. They are really conspirators in disguise, who succour the weak-hearted, raise up them that fall, and would finally beat down the Sultan under their feet. They have done much to help the Armenian refugees from Turkey; have concealed men, clothed and fed them, and have generally aided and abetted the revolutionary movement to the utmost of their power, especially by exhortation and precept. Of course the influence of the clergy is incalculably great. They have many difficulties to contend with, for the spies of the Russian Government are at their heels, and watch their every movement. Yet they are bold and stout-hearted, not the least striking of their characteristics is their lofty contempt for the police, and the courage with which they devote themselves to the cause in exceptionally difficult circumstances.

One thing my visit to Etchmiadzin made me sure of, and that was that the Armenian clergy were possessed of a deep-rooted conviction that the Russian Government was determined to undermine, and if possible abolish, their religion, and I felt that their hatred of "ungrateful" Russia was only one degree less intense than their detestation of the "Great Assassin."

These tall gaunt figures, in their sombre black robes, and quaint hoods, impressed me very strongly. I felt that here was a force which Sultan and Tzar would be alike unable to conquer, and which might yet accomplish the salvation of the Armenian race. They were emphatically members of the Church militant.

Altogether I spent a most interesting day at Etchmiadzin, and among the sights I saw, the printing works of the monastery did not seem to me to be the least important. The monastery prints and publishes its own journal. In the photographic studio of this religious retreat, where the modern and the ancient world are so strangely blended, I purchased a photograph of the Catholicos, a reproduction of which accompanies the present volume.

I inspected the schools, and saw the intelligent Armenian boys, though the time was not a favourable one, for the Easter holidays were in full swing. Nevertheless, several Armenian boys, who had no homes to go to, were staying on at the monastery.

Finally, I had tea with the monks, and then drove back to Erivan, just as the sun was setting. The monks rather speedied my departure, for they told me the roads, especially in the vicinity of Erivan, were very unsafe. I am bound to say that on my return journey, and as darkness was coming on, I met several very unpleasant-looking characters, but no adventures occurred to give an air of romance to this very matter-of-fact recital of what I saw and heard.

Arrived at Erivan, I met at the post-house one of those strange characters which abound throughout Russia and the East. He was a German piano-tuner, who had come to Erivan to tune the pianos of the Governor-General and the aristocracy. Bibulous and communicative, he was a most amusing fellow, full of

R

stories of bribery and corruption, and of his exploits among the fair sex.

These piano-tuners are people of great importance. On my journey to Resht, a broken down Russian officer, a charming fellow, came on board at Linkoran and tuned the ship's piano. He was taken over to Resht gratis, and I shall never forget the sight of him, mounted on a Persian horse and galloping from Pir-Bazaar. At Resht he tuned the pianos of the English and Russian Consuls, as well as of the Greek, and gave a concert at the residence of the Russian Consul, and was made a great fuss of. He had a glorious time, and was, I believe, drunk for one entire month at Resht.

When I arrived at Erivan, I confess to feeling considerable anxiety about my passport. It had not been returned. The diligence would start next morning, and I wanted to be out of Erivan and well on my way to Tiflis, for I had come here in open violation of the express prohibition of the Russian Government, which had been communicated to me by the Governor-General of the Caucasus at Tiflis.

" How about my passport ? " I asked of my funny Armenian inn-keeper friend.

" That will be all right, sir. I will look after that."

" Well, look here, I want it now, and if you will get it for me I will give you five roubles."

That worked like a charm, and sure enough that

evening I got my passport, so that there was now nothing to prevent my journeying by diligence next day.

The diligence drive was very amusing ; we had strange passengers, of all sorts, and it took the best part of a week ; but we drove through beautiful scenery—scenery of every description, mountain and forest. I certainly got a very good sight of the Caucasus, and was impressed with its gigantic undeveloped resources. Here is a great country running to waste for want of intelligent workers and a wise administration.

Wherever I came across settlements of Russian dissenters, or Armenian villages, I saw prosperity and cheerfulness ; but the Circassian indigenous population are hopelessly slothful.

One of the most interesting spots I passed was Lake Sevan, famous for its fish and its monastery, which is situated on a bare and bleak island. The climate on Lake Sevan, which is situated on a table-land, is particularly severe, and hither are sent for punishment such naughty Armenian monks as have misbehaved themselves ; it is, in short, the Siberia of Etchmiadzin.

When finally our diligence drove up at the railway-station, we learned that a train had recently been attacked and robbed by a band of Circassian robbers. Life in the Caucasus is still therefore far from safe.

Among my fellow-passengers was a lady, the wife

of a Russian colonel stationed in the Caucasus, and it was interesting to hear her chat. I made friends with this lady, and elicited from her, in the course of conversation, that her daughters were being educated at the expense of the State; her sons also, in reward for certain services her husband had rendered; but she had many grievances, the greatest being the expense of the coronation. Her husband had been compelled to purchase a new uniform, and had spent a lot of money at St. Petersburg.

CHAPTER XIII.

THE RUSSIAN SHORES OF THE BLACK SEA.

IMMEDIATELY on my arrival at the station of the Trans-Caucasian Railway, I took my ticket for Batoum, and when, some four hours later, the train actually steamed in, I took my seat and did not think of breaking my journey at Tiflis. Having defied the Russian Government successfully so far, I was not going to court disaster now.

At Batoum I had a narrow escape from travelling to England in a petroleum-tank steamer. I was introduced to the captain of this malodorous vessel, a typical British tar, by our Consul at Batoum, and the idea of becoming his passenger struck me as original. But wiser counsels prevailed, and I took my ticket for Odessa at the offices of the Russian Steamboat Company.

In the last chapter I described my unprepossessing appearance and costume. I need only add that my journey by diligence and train, during the whole of which time I had been unable to wash, had not improved me; but the sensual man has fleshly appetites. It was a considerable period since I had had a really comfortable and palatable square meal, and I knew from experience that the cooking at the Hôtel de France at Batoum was excellent. So, all grimy, uncouth, unwashed, and unshaven, I walked into the restaurant of this swagger hostelry. Seated at one of the tables I espied a French gentleman, the business manager of a large firm in the Caucasus, and the personal friend of the newly-appointed Governor of Batoum, whose acquaintance I had made at Tiflis. This gentleman was lunching with an eminently respectable friend. I walked up to him and asked him how he was. He shrank back, looked horrified, and assured me that I had the advantage of him. But when I told him who I was and recalled to him the circumstances under which I had been introduced to him at Tiflis, he burst into a roar of laughter, and told me he would not have known me anywhere, but had taken me for a sturdy beggar, who was on the point of asking for alms. Highly gratified at this sincere and genuine compliment, I partook of a capital luncheon and proceeded to the steamer, which, luckily for me, was to leave that night. It was a magnificent and luxuriously appointed vessel, with electric light and every comfort. It might have challenged comparison with the ocean palaces which ply between Europe and America, and in the matter of cuisine it was vastly superior to them. I felt like a disembodied spirit, which, after the trials of a life in this sublunary world, had at length been admitted into heaven!

One of my fellow-travellers was a colonel of Cossacks, invalided home. He had the cross of St. George for valour, and had been one of Skobeleff's officers, serving under him in the Russo-Turkish war, and at Geok-Teppé. I soon fraternised with this genial hero, who was as honest and unsophisticated as a child, and a splendid fellow in every respect. He told me his life history, which was a very chequered one, and his misfortunes and troubles. How he had gone to the devil, and then pulled himself together, and was now about to retire to his estates, and end his days peacefully in the bosom of his family. He was a man of good family, had been educated at the aristocratic *Corps des Pages* in St. Petersburg, and knew Russian society and Court life thoroughly, but had a manly contempt for its rottenness. He was also a pronounced antagonist of priestcraft. He had a brother an admiral, and other relations all enjoying brilliant positions. Altogether, he was a typical Russian officer of the old school, and reminded me of some of the noble characters to be met with in Turgueniev's novels.

The scenery was magnificent. As our vessel steamed away from Batoum, and the mountains of the Caucasus receded from us, we could see the snow-capped peaks of that glorious range meeting the deep blue sky above. Under the snow-capped mountains lay a tier of smaller hills covered with smiling verdure, then came a belt of forests, for the shores of the Caspian are well-wooded, and this was fringed by a border of yellow sand terminating in the dark blue of the Black Sea. The colour effect was superb.

As we steamed along, stopping at every port, I had opportunities of studying the pleasant patriarchal methods of government which still prevail. But from the confidences of the owner of a sawmill, a French pioneer of industry on the Caucasus, I discovered that life was not so easy and charming as it appeared on surface. This Frenchman is opening up a big trade with France, and exports to Paris large quantities of long strips of rare woods which are used for veneering purposes. He had also purchased wood-working machinery, and produced numbers of carvings which in Paris were fitted to furniture. This simple trade, perfectly straightforward and uncomplicated one would imagine, had aroused the covetousness and jealousy of the officials, and the way this Frenchman had been bled, if all his accounts were true, was marvellous. In all sorts of petty ways had the local Jacks-in-office tried to hamper him, often with considerable success. They took the part of his work-people against him. They tried to control him in innumerable ways ; in short, he was getting very sick and tired of life in Russia. Yet he was a Frenchman, and the authorities are supposed to look on France, and all that comes from there, with loving eyes. But it is always the same story. The Russian official dreads progress of all kinds, for the same reason that the Psalmist says men prefer the darkness to the day, because their works are evil. The commercial and lower classes, on the other hand, are still so backward in their economic education that they look with eyes of hatred on all enterprises which enrich their neighbours. The Russian mind argues that if a man has acquired wealth it must have been at the expense of his neighbours, and it cannot understand that the rich producer, or industrial capitalist must, by the very condition of his continued prosperity, be a centre of distribution. Wealth makes wealth. This the average Russian mind cannot understand.

Another scourge of this unfortunate Frenchman was the brigands who infested the richly timbered forests of the Caucasus. These brigands were mostly in league with the police, as I have already pointed out, and used to attack his clerks and travellers, whom he would send to purchase timber, and who had to carry the money with them, for banking operations are still but imperfectly understood in these regions.

The Cossack colonel also told me that most of the Cossacks settled in the Caucasus were brigands.

" Splendid fellows ! " he said. " Plucky scoundrels, who won't work, but value their lives as little as I do this cigarette. Those chaps will never be tamed."

The first place of interest, to me at least, which we touched was the monastery of New Athens. This monastery, which is situated picturesquely on a hill overlooking the sea, is partly buried in trees. There are about one hundred and fifty monks in this place, who live on the fat of the land, and are kept flourishing by the contribution of pilgrims from all parts of Russia. As our steamer stopped at some distance from this holy place, whose respectable antiquity does not date farther back than 1875, crowds of steerage passengers came on deck and demanded to be allowed to land. They wore every variety of national costume, and made a highly picturesque group. Presently clumsy barges were seen to put off from the shore ; they were rowed by monks, in quaint-looking velvet sugar-loaf caps, long hair streaming down their shoulders, and long cloaks. As they came alongside I could see that they were revoltingly filthy to look at, and had the most evil faces I ever gazed upon. Such a contrast to the intelligent monks of Etchmiadzin.

My Cossack friend drew my attention to them and said : "Aren't they disgusting ? Until I saw them I thought it would be a good thing to be a monk. Nothing to do, plenty to eat and drink, and no worries —a glorious life. The disgusting, loathsome rascals ! "

I find that although the monastery was not commenced until 1875, and not completed until 1879, there is, nevertheless, an ancient ruin of a church in the neighbourhood, from which the place derives its sanctity.

The Cossack colonel now discovered to his alarm that several priests were going to honour us with their company as first-class fellow-passengers, and he was beside himself with rage. He told me we should all be alive with vermin, and asked me to consider the vileness and sinister cast of the countenances of these priests. I must in truthfulness admit that I did not see reflected on the impassive faces of these stolid recluses the evidences of an exceptional malignity of heart within. They struck me more as lazy and stupid, from whose eyes the light of intelligence had departed, if, indeed, it had ever illuminated them, and who were good-natured, self-indulgent, and slothful, rather than actively wicked.

But the Cossack colonel would not hear of my defence of these harmless parasites of a superstitious peasantry.

"They are the curse of the country," he said ; "they have made progress impossible, and they are becoming powerful and insolent."

The next place of interest at which we stopped was Novorossisk. This is the new granary of the Black Sea. It has been created and fostered by the Government in order to weaken Odessa, which the ruling powers hate for its large foreign population, its intelligence, and its liberal aspirations. Odessa is regarded as the home of the Jew and the Greek, and as a sort of commercial ulcer, which has been sapping the vitals of the Russian commonwealth, and is under-

mining the integrity of the honest Russian people.
But a curious thing occurred here. A gentleman
came on board who turned out to be the head of a
famous firm of Jewish grain merchants, whose business
offices were in former times situated at Odessa, and
whose name was, as it afterwards turned out, wrong-
fully held up to opprobrium during the famine year
of 1892. As a matter of fact, his firm was made
responsible for the peculations and malfaisance of the
Russian railway officials, and its honour was subsequently fully vindicated. It was the celebrated
firm of Dreyfus and Co., which practically monopolised
the grain trade of the Black Sea. To-day it is still
bravely fighting against adverse circumstances, and,
now that the grain trade has been deflected from
Odessa to Novorossisk and Kertch, it has established
branches and agencies all along the Black Sea. So
that the authorities have not after all succeeded in
turning out the great Jewish commercial houses of the
south. In fact, if they did, there would be nobody
to take their place. The grain trade of Russia is
languishing, but this is due not to the tricky and
avaricious methods of the great Jewish firms, but to
many causes. New countries have been opened out of
late years ; Hungary, Canada, America, the Argentine
Republic, and India are competing with Russia in the
grain markets of the world. This competition is all
the more keenly felt because, as I had occasion to
point out in a book I published in 1892, entitled ; " In

the Track of the Russian Famine," the Russian producers are dishonest ; they do not deliver to sample,
and their grain is inferior to that of other countries
by reason of its adulteration with gravel, sand, and
similar ingredients. This is a melancholy state of
things for which the great Jewish export houses can
scarcely be held responsible.

At Novorossisk there is an enormous grain-elevator,
of which the Russians are inordinately proud. Here
the railway systems of Russia meet, and it is a much
more convenient port for that reason than Odessa.
But all the efforts of the Government to stimulate it
into commercial activity have proved of questionable
value. The town looks desolate and moribund.
Russian enterprise and business ability is a minus
quantity unless stimulated by foreigners, as in Moscow
for instance. Hence the policy of the Government to
keep the foreigner out has had melancholy results.
For all that there is visible all over the south of
Russia a sort of surface activity which will deceive the
traveller. He will see railways, harbours, telephones,
telegraphs, and all the evidences of modern industrialism, and will hastily conclude that Russia is
a thriving young giant ; but these indications of
industrial life are deceptive. They are mostly fostered
by the State and have no real vitality ; they can
scarcely be said to have been created by popular
demand or native enterprise.

The Russian is at heart an official. His great idea

is to get a good Government post and retire on a
comfortable pension with the money which he has
accumulated in questionable ways. But he regards
with suspicion all commercial enterprise, and is too
much in the habit of denouncing all classes of
merchants and traders as thieves and scoundrels.

Thus we see that the natural products of Russian
life are the official, the soldier, and the priest, who live
on the people. The Russian middle classes are
educated in this direction. Their sole ambition is
to "serve the State," and Russia is a large country
with enormous tracts of land inhabited by an ignorant
and semi-civilised peasantry, and for the administration
of these tracts of land educated officials are required.
The Government of Russia is a sort of socialistic
despotism, in which the State does everything and
the individual nothing; indeed, the individual is discouraged from doing the little that he seems to do.

From Novorossisk we proceeded to Kertch, and
then continued our voyage along the smiling shores
of the soft and luxuriant Crimea, the Riviera of
Russia. Here we definitely bade farewell to the
grand scenery of the Caucasus, whose retreating
shores had kept in sight for an incredibly long time.
We stopped at Yalta and passed Livadia, the scene of
the last days of the late Emperor, Alexander III., and
now we got into Balaklava.

"Here we shall catch it," said my Cossack friend.
"The sea is always rough at Balaklava."

It was appropriately just before luncheon.

"That is to remind you fellows of us," I said, grimly, at which the Cossack laughed very good-naturedly. Just off the Balaklava Heights I looked up and saw the Balaklava monument, and I thought of that terrible day when the British army saw from those heights the transports, laden with the supplies and the warm clothing they so much needed, dash themselves to pieces against the rocks before their very eyes.

As we steamed into Sevastopol Harbour we saw unfolded before us the imposing panorama of the Black Sea Fleet; but when we got nearer to the individual vessels I was surprised at the bad condition in which they appeared to be. Their sides were sadly in need of paint, and they looked dirty and out of repair. There was no neatness or smartness about them. The discipline seemed slack, the yards were badly trimmed, and there was a general happy-go-lucky air about everything.

There was a stoppage of several hours at Sevastopol, and so I went on shore to look at the town; but there was no time to go to see the cemetery. I am bound to say that in my walk round the town I experienced no annoyance of any kind, and I was surprised to learn later from the papers that a party of English gentlemen had not been allowed to land.

Although it is about forty years ago since the Crimean War, Sevastopol still looks as though it had but recently emerged from a siege. In the new and handsome streets there are countless ruins. Rows of shattered barracks are still standing. Everywhere the eye meets evidences of the severity of the bombardment. Side by side with these crumbling mementoes of the past are the noble promises of the future, really beautiful public buildings, severely classical in style and white and new, pretty parks, broad boulevards. Altogether Sevastopol is a beautiful city; nevertheless, it looks as though an invading army had passed through it but yesterday. Lest the people of Russia should be blind to the ruins which still remain standing, and forget the lessons they teach, the Government has erected a number of museums in which the history of Russian prowess and of Russian reverses is treasured for the edification of future generations. Close to these national treasure-houses are the forts to protect them, and at the foot of the city, which is built on a hill, in the spacious harbour, are riding at anchor the frowning battleships, which will prevent, it is believed, a repetition of history.

The population of Sevastopol seems to consist principally of naval officers, tradespeople, and very gorgeously-attired ladies. I was subsequently informed that the naval officers of Sevastopol are the terror of the tradespeople. Those whom I saw were fine strapping fellows, but I am assured that they are dissipated and impecunious; besides, the life is

extravagant, and they are not as a rule wealthy.
Nevertheless, they are very much underpaid. As a
protection to the tradespeople the authorities frequently administer the debts of these young officers.
What happens is, I am told, this : A tradesman will
complain in the right quarter that a certain officer
owes him money for goods delivered, and cannot be
induced to pay. The authorities will thereupon stop
a certain proportion of the officer's pay until the debt
is liquidated. In the case of several tradespeople
coming together a similar course is adopted. When
it is remembered that the average pay of a Russian
sub-lieutenant does not amount to more than about
five pounds a month, and that very often that is all
he has to live on, people will understand what this
means. Necessarily the dare-devil Russian officer,
who is generally a gambler and an admirer of the fair
sex, besides being a sworn foe to total abstainers, is
heavily in debt by the time he gets a responsible
command. Is it surprising that he should endeavour
to retrieve his fortunes at the expense of the State ?
Besides, everybody does it. There is even a pretty
little word for peculation in Russia ; it is called
"economy." An officer who has never been known
to exercise that virtue on himself may prove a wonderful practitioner of economy where the State is concerned. The Russian navy is not more free from
abuses and corruption than any other branch of the
Russian service, and presents more opportunities.

S

For this reason the stores and ammunition are open to grave suspicion.

The Russian navy is composed of a guard and a line, and, while our navy is stated to be under-manned, the reverse may be said to be the case with the Russian. All the great naval stations, including St. Petersburg, have enormous blocks of barracks, where the sailors who are not away on active service are housed, drilled, and trained. They are mostly tall, powerful fellows, a little heavy and awkward perhaps, and generally pale-faced. They are fed principally on black bread and porridge, have no end of endurance, wear heavy, long-heeled boots up to their knees, and are not smart, nor even tidy in appearance. Of their intelligence the less said the better. They are simply fine raw material. Well fed, well groomed, and well led, they would do anything; but whether their officers have sufficient self-restraint and education to mould them into what we should call able seamen is very doubtful. There can be no question but that these officers are of a superior class to that from which the officers of the Russian infantry of the line are drawn, but whether their technical knowledge is abreast of the times is a different matter. For brilliant cutting out expeditions the Russian naval officer is eminently fitted, and during the last Russo-Turkish war the Russian navy proved itself to be possessed of dash and pluck; but these qualities were manifested by the torpedo service.

The managing, fighting, and manœuvring of large battleships is not quite the same thing.

We have been told repeatedly that the Russian Black Sea Fleet is ready to steam into the Bosphorus on the shortest notice ; but very few of the vessels I saw were fit to go into action.

I made the acquaintance on the way to Odessa of an English engineer who had been engaged on some Russian battleships, and was going home for his holiday. He was thoroughly acquainted with the condition of the Russian navy. It is curious that the Russian Government is obliged to get English engineers to work for them. But the reason for this was explained to me.

" They have no good engineers," the Englishman said. " The Russian engineers do not know their work and cannot be trusted. They often spoil and break machinery, and are then unable to mend it. Besides, they very frequently allow steering and other gear to rust."

" That is very bad, is it not ? " I inquired.

" Yes," he replied. " I do not know what would happen to the Russian navy if it had really to fight. I think it would go to pieces for want of technical knowledge. They do not understand their machinery."

" It strikes me," I said, " that the Black Sea Fleet does not seem to be in an efficient state of repair."

" Of course not," he answered. " It is rotting for want of paint. The commanding officers steal the money for the paint and the ships have to go without. You should see their bottoms !"

" Why ?   What is the matter with them ? "

" They are nearly all rotten.   You see, the water of the Black Sea has a peculiar corroding action on copper, and the vessels must be turned up and painted periodically to protect them.   But this cannot be done when a ship is fully fitted out ; and do you know how long it takes to fit out a Russian man-of-war ?   Four years after she is delivered !   They are so slow, and such thieves !   It is nobody's interest to hurry."

This staggered me.

" Yes," he continued, " and by that time her bottom is completely corroded by the action of the water of the Black Sea."

" Then the Black Sea Fleet is only formidable on paper ? "

" That is about it.   It is a fine fleet, but it is not fit to go anywhere.   Besides, the officers and men are a seedy drunken lot ! "

This was a somewhat sweeping statement, but, allowing perhaps for a little exaggeration, it was not far from the truth.   A pretty severe indictment it was of the Russian navy.

Odessa is probably the most beautiful city in the dominions of the Tzar—it is certainly the prettiest that I have seen.   The town itself is situated on a plateau commanding the harbour, which is of grand dimensions and full of shipping. At night the lights of Nikolaieff are just visible in the distance. Fronting the town, and commanding a splendid view of the harbour, is a series of spacious boulevards, beautifully laid out. Here are band-stands where the bands of the various regiments stationed at Odessa discourse sweet music at night. There are restaurants with gardens overlooking the harbour on these boulevards, and here of an evening come the citizens of Odessa, with their wives and daughters, to sip lemonade or drink mild beer, listen to the band, and look down on the harbour brightly illuminated with electric light. The ladies of Odessa are remarkable for the elegance of their toilettes and their voluptuous beauty. Altogether these boulevards present a gay and brilliant spectacle. From the principal of these there is a grand flight of granite steps leading straight down into the harbour, a distance of several hundred feet.

The public buildings of Odessa are magnificent. The town-hall is a beautiful and severely classical Greek temple built of white marble. The theatre is a replica of the Grande Opéra at Paris. The streets are wide, shops plentiful and handsome, the hotels excellent. In short, Odessa is a splendid modern city, with substantially built private houses and every indication of wealth, but it owes its prosperity mainly to its own enterprise. It is the foreign merchants of Odessa who have made her what she is ; the great Greek and Jewish houses. Polished, enlightened and

educated, the citizens of Odessa have ever been in
sympathy with the liberal aspirations of Russia. They
have little in common with the narrow spirit of a
"zoological patriotism," as Professor Solovieff designated it, which has animated the ruling powers of late.
They cannot understand the fanatic Slavophilism of
the new school of Russian patriots, and think that
education and commercial enterprise are better
calculated to help on the progress of a great country
with vast natural resources than the shibboleths of
mystic dreamers. For this reason Odessa is regarded
as a disintegrating force in the Russian empire, as
unpatriotic, as disaffected, and hence the Government
is doing all in its power to deflect from Odessa the
trade which used formerly to flow to it.

This policy has only been partially successful.
Odessa still is, and will probably always remain, the
commercial capital of the south of Russia, notwithstanding the fact that Kieff is the headquarters of the
military district, and Novorossisk, as we have seen,
the depot of the grain trade.

The enterprising and wily Greek and Jewish merchants of Odessa are likely to make a stubborn fight
for their commercial existence ; they are resourceful,
self-reliant, and wealthy, and moreover educated.
Nevertheless the town of Odessa is feeling the consequences of the distrust of the Government, and
complaining of bad trade. The good old times have
passed, it is said, and all that people can do is to live.

The days of money-making are over. I am inclined to think, from the evidences of the prosperity which I saw, that this is an unduly pessimistic view. Undoubtedly Odessa is participating in the bad times which have come over the entire trade of Russia. The decline of the grain trade, to which I have already referred, is only one of numerous factors in the commercial depression of Russia. One of the principal reasons for this decline of Russian trade is undoubtedly purely fiscal, and must be sought in the rise of the exchange value of the rouble. That rise has been caused by no appreciable improvement in the financial condition of Russia, in the solvency of her peasantry, or in the increase of productive work. It is due entirely to cleverly manipulated loan operations on the bourses of Europe, by means of which Russia has been able to reduce the interest on her debt, and to perform certain gymnastics in the world of *haute finance*, the utility of which has been very great to her financiers, but is very doubtful for the country. When the prices of her exports are raised on the markets of the world by a rise in the exchange value of her currency, but the purchasing power of that currency has not been proportionately increased, but has rather declined within its own frontiers, a country is necessarily very much hampered in its competition with other countries. In other words, while the rouble will buy no more in Russia than formerly, but rather less, its exchange value has been artificially raised. This may be clever finance, and must have benefited a great many astute gentlemen in Paris and St. Petersburg, but it can hardly be looked upon as a cause for congratulation for the nation. Besides, Russian trade is not based on such solid and firm foundations as to be able to afford such handicapping. We must not forget that Russian trade and prosperity are not based upon her manufacturing industries, or her mineral exports, but upon the peasant. But the Russian peasant is in a state verging upon bankruptcy. He is impoverished beyond the conception of European economists, his taxes are hopelessly in arrear, he is visited by periodic famines, and he is kept in a state of ignorance and backwardness verging on barbarism.

Yet it is the Russian peasant who must eventually pay for everything. But his condition is not much better than that of the French peasant before the French Revolution, so graphically described by Arthur Young in 1787-1789, and though he has to find the soldiers and sailors that shall carry out the schemes for aggrandisement of his statesmen, pays the salaries of all those statesmen and their armies of officials, pays for her railways, for the ships, for everything, and is robbed right and left, a limit must be reached, a time will come when he will no longer be able to bear his ever increasing load, and the moment of breaking strain will be reached.

From Odessa I returned home, *via* Kieff, Warsaw, and Berlin. Kieff, the ancient capital of Russia, with its magnificent river and its wonderful old monastery, is a strange object lesson of the present condition of Russia. While on the one hand I saw long trains of pilgrims coming on foot from villages a thousand miles distant, and bringing their humble donations to enrich the coffers of the rich and indolent priests, who live upon the credulity and benightedness of the masses, I found that all the commercial enterprise of this very progressive city was in the hands of Jews and Poles—a melancholy testimony to the incapacity for business of the pure Russian.

And the contrast between the villages of Russia, poverty-stricken and untidy, and the neatness of the fields of Poland! Then again, on crossing the Russian frontier into Germany I experienced very much the same feeling which I did when I arrived at Batoum from Trebizond. Here were civilisation, order, and energy. The very atmosphere was different.

CHAPTER XIV.

HAVING concluded my rambles "round about Armenia," and recorded them to the best of my ability, however faultily and incompletely, I propose now to connect the threads of my story and to ask the reader who has patiently followed me from Constantinople to Tiflis, and from Tiflis across Northern Persia to Etchmiadzin and Warsaw, to bear with me yet a little longer while I endeavour to reproduce as well as I am able the general impression left upon my mind of the Armenian question.

That question is full of interest to all thinking people, and to many emotional temperaments who do not think at all. But, before talking about Armenia, let us define it. It is a much more important country than is generally supposed, and may be conveniently called the Switzerland of the East. Within its confines stands Mount Ararat, and it forms a sort of cushion between Turkey, Persia and Russia. To-day it is a kind of Poland—indeed its population have

many of the characteristics of the Poles—and it is
omnia divisa in partes tres : Turkish Armenia, Russian
Armenia, and Persian Armenia.   If we push the comparison further, we may liken Russian Armenia, with
Kars and Etchmiadzin, the ancient cathedral and
seat of the Catholicos, to Austrian Poland, with its
Cracow ; Turkish Armenia, with Erzeroum, the
capital, to Russian Poland, which retains Warsaw ;
and Persian Armenia to German Poland, for there
the Armenians appear to have most liberty.

But comparisons are odious.   What is interesting
is that Armenia is a natural buffer state between
three countries, who are inimical one to the other.
For Turkey cannot hate Russia more than she does
Persia, and Russia's appetite for Constantinople, and
for absolute dominion in the Black Sea, can only be
equalled by her longing for a port in the Persian Gulf,
and her determination to make the Caspian Sea an
integral part of her Empire.   Unless something unforeseen occurs, Russia must, from the sheer force of
circumstances, eventually swallow, even though she
may never be able to digest, both Turkey and Persia.
Will Armenia develop into this unforeseen something ?
That is the question which British statesmen have to
ask themselves.

When regarded in this light, and in connection with
the surrounding political facts, the Armenian question
assumes a peculiarly interesting aspect for English
people.

In the present case it is very easy to lose sight of the forests of fact for the trees of incidents of which these facts are constituted.

We cannot too much honour the noble sympathy and enthusiasm which the British public—which has ever befriended oppressed nationalities—has manifested for the unfortunate victims of human or, rather, fiendish cruelty. But the cynical "practical politicians" are ever repeating to us that mere sentiment is out of place in the game of international politics.

As early as February 6th, 1895, I said in the *Daily Graphic*, foreseeing this probable attitude of the Philistines :—

"Whatever the truth may be, one factor must not be omitted, and that is diplomacy. High diplomatic considerations are very mysterious, but after all it is questionable whether the lives of two hundred, or even twenty thousand Armenians, are worth risking the lives of millions for, and it is quite possible that the maintenance of peace in Europe may be of greater importance to humanity than the security of Armenia."

These words were prophetic. Let us purge our minds of sentiment, and endeavour to take a calm, common-sense and self-interested view of the situation.

I know that will be difficult for many people. The massacres are a fact, and although I have described only those of Sassun, the public need not be reminded that they were but the commencement of a series of atrocities spread over the length and breadth of this once smiling and prosperous land of Turkish Armenia. The foulness of the deeds perpetrated in the name of the Sultan, and at his express behest—for nothing is done in Turkey without the Sultan, as I have shown— is so great, so horrible, that no pen would consent to write them down in all their obscene particulars, no self-respecting publisher would give them to the world. Imagination pales before the diabolical ingenuity of these persecutions. The wildest fiction would not come near the terrible realities of the truth.

For this reason I have abstained from dwelling upon the lurid details of the massacres. They convince nobody, they seem too horrible to be true, and hence those faithful scribes who have reported them, in part only, of course, in our daily papers have been accused of exaggeration and falsehood. But these details have been confirmed in the sober language of the official reports of our consuls. For some time the Government hesitated in having these reports printed. I have myself seen the unprinted MSS. of some of them, and their perusal made my blood run cold.

Face to face with those horrors it is almost impossible to discuss the question calmly and prudently. But it is absolutely indispensable, in the very interests of the persecuted Armenians themselves, that we should divest ourselves of all passion, and look the whole problem fairly and squarely in the face.

We have to ask ourselves this question: "Is it England's duty to succour these Armenians, and to do so even in the face of the united millions of armed Europe ? "

That question honourable and upright men can only answer in the affirmative, and unless England has lost her manhood, become a craven nation, and is no more worthy of her great empire, she must answer it in the same way. Who of us seeing a boy, a woman or other helpless person, nay even an animal, brutally used by some ruffian, would not step in and defend the victim ? It is the duty of humanity to protect the weak, and it is the duty of everybody professing or calling himself Christian.

Unfortunately, however, we shall be met on the very threshold of our argument by the cynical Philistines, who will tell us that this is all foolish sentiment, and that it is not worth while risking the continued existence of the British Empire for the sake of a few Armenians. This seems an extreme statement of the views of the party for non-intervention, but it is nevertheless the argument which has been publicly set forth in the press.

It so happens, however, that this reasoning is fallacious. It is not true that intervention would endanger the British Empire ; I do not even believe it would disturb the peace of Europe. But if we allow things to go on as they are, that would indeed endanger our future, and embolden the Powers to carry out still further their notable policy of thwarting England.

That the Powers of Europe are bent on crippling, and if possible ruining, England is no mere nightmare, the foolish fancy of alarmists. It is the determined policy of three great countries, Russia, Germany, and France. Prince Bismarck was the successor of Napoleon the Great in his active hatred of England, and to-day the German Emperor and M. Hanotaux are at one on this point. Of the attitude of Russia it is needless to speak.

In 1894 I was for a short period the resident correspondent in Paris of a great American paper, and had frequent occasion to visit the Quai d'Orsay, with the officials of which I was on pleasant and friendly terms.

One day, while I was calling on the chief of a department, the card of a French diplomatist from the Far East was brought in.

"That is a man you should see," said the chief of department; "he is most interesting and very clever."

I was therefore introduced to this gentleman, and we had a long and, to me at least, most instructive conversation, at the end of which he concluded with the words:

" *Vous verrez, au bout de quelques ans il n'y aura plus d'Angleterre !*"

In the spring or summer of 1895 it will be remembered that a French paper predicted that the Egyptian question was going to be brought up for definite settlement in the autumn. A cabinet crisis

in France prevented the execution of these plans.
M. Hanotaux was out of office, and M. Bertholet, a
man of great scientific attainments, was not quite up
to date in his diplomatic methods.

Of the brilliant and dazzling career of Prince
Lobanoff-Rostovski, who flashed like a comet across
the firmament of diplomacy, it has been said that
its dominating feature was hatred of England.

The recently published letter of Prince Bismarck to
his royal master, commenting on the Queen's despatch
to the German Emperor in 1875, sufficiently betrays
that statesman's animus towards England, if additional
indications were wanted. But his cynical confession
that he encouraged England to go to Egypt in order
to create difficulties for her, published some years
ago, places his policy in so strong a light that
all supplementary testimony is superfluous. The
present German Emperor has shown that he did
not sit at the feet of the Iron Chancellor for so
many years without imbibing his prejudices.

The simple-minded, unthinking " man in the street "
is for ever expressing his surprise at the hostility of
the " foreigner " towards us, and in club smoking-
rooms it is the fashion to attribute to our insular
angularity the hatred of the Continent.

For my part, and I have lived a great deal on the
Continent, I am constrained to wonder at this hasty
conclusion. The " insular angularity," which was
once the favourite theme of the comic papers of

France, made us respected, if it did not make us beloved, and has been copied all over Europe, but, strange to say, we ourselves have successfully and definitely rubbed it off.

I am willing to admit that very frequently our statesmen, educated in the arena of party politics, have assumed the reins of the Foreign Office with too scanty an equipment of diplomatic training. But although this may have been true of Lord Palmerston and his school, it cannot be predicated either of Lord Granville, Lord Rosebery, or Lord Salisbury.

There must be other causes at work to produce this universal jealousy of England. That jealousy is not a thing of yesterday. It has existed from time immemorial. Without exaggeration the student of history may say that every new century brings England face to face with new dangers, or with a powerful combination threatening to the continuance of her national life.

To go no farther back than the days of Queen Elizabeth, we find the Powers of Europe, divided though they were amongst themselves, united in one thing, hatred of England, and that condition was not altered at the accession of Queen Anne, the close of the eighteenth century, or during the prosperous reign of Queen Victoria.

For a great deal of this jealousy we have to thank our geographical position, which, while it has made us independent of the rest of Europe, has enabled

T

us always to pursue steadily our own policy, to harass our neighbours, and to throw the weight of our power, influence, and wealth in the scales on behalf of any country whom we chose to befriend without reference to the political calculations of Europe.

In other words, England has been a disturbing element in the councils of Europe. Her interests have never been identical with those of other Powers for any considerable time, and her possessions beyond the seas have been factors in her calculations which the rest of Europe was frequently unable to clearly understand.

Our geographical position has led to our assuming the command of the sea, to our carrying our adventurous sons into distant and undiscovered countries, there to settle and form new Englands. We have thus put a girdle of English settlements round the earth, we have peopled three continents, we govern a large part of a fourth, and, outside Europe, no country is of any consequence by the side of England.

European countries, jealous of our achievements, are endeavouring to imitate our example. But they find that, while on the one hand the principal squatting-grounds of the habitable globe have already been "coralled" by the Anglo-Saxon race, Continental races have not, on the other, the ability of colonising those that remain.

The futile efforts of Germany and France to build up colonies in Asia and Africa would be ludicrous if they were not so pathetic.

Besides giving us colonies, our geographical position gave us trade. Modern research seems to have established that the history of English trade is practically coincident with that of England. England has ever, protected by the silver streak, followed the peaceful arts of industry and trade, whereas her less fortunate Continental neighbours have spent a great part of their time in defending themselves against each other.

With the new era of modern civilisation the wealth of nations became the first solicitude of statesmen. Napoleon III. and Prince Bismarck have, it is not too much to say, created the capitalism of Europe.

Hedged in by protective tariffs, the Continent has produced manufactures as grapes are produced in a hothouse, and before the wealth of the masses had progressed sufficiently to create a demand for them within their own frontier. The necessary consequence is that melancholy disease of our modern industrialism, called over-production.

A large class of wealthy manufacturers has been artificially produced by these means, but, coincidently therewith, the civilised world has now got a much larger class of underpaid, discontented slaves, factory-hands, whose methods of wage-earning have led to the disruption of family ties, the demoralisation of large numbers of the community, and to the formulation of a new theory of life called "Socialism."

Foreign countries, in imitating the example of England, have created for themselves a Frankenstein, which they dread, but which they cannot kill.

To provide food for this hungry monster they are seeking for new markets, but wherever they go they are confronted by British trade, British enterprise, and British perseverance. However they may deceive themselves, they generally find in the long run that by their insensate competition they are harming themselves much more than they are injuring us.

With Socialism and discontent in their midst, heavy armaments to maintain, and an ever-increasing national expenditure, the countries of Europe turn their eyes to England and see that we are comparatively free from the burdens which are well-nigh bearing them down. Owing to our peculiar institutions, our habits of sport and freedom, we have developed a national character which is resourceful and patient, practical, and comparatively constant.

We cannot understand their fear of revolution, for in our country revolutions are frequent, peaceful, and automatic. We cannot follow their political combinations, for we have no need of them. The English people, from time immemorial, have been accustomed to help themselves, and to distrust the State. Necessarily, our whole methods of thought and bent of mind are totally different.

But the countries of Europe dread our increasing power, they dread the fearless force of a nation which has ever hated tyranny, no matter of what kind, and which is to-day, by its moral and intellectual influence, slowly conquering the world.

Do not let us deceive ourselves—it is futile to hope that the military despotisms of Europe, for they are nothing else, whatever their outward forms of government may be, will ever become the friends and allies of England.

These general considerations are not new, they are familiar to all who have studied the history of modern Europe ; but it is necessary that we should focus them, so that we may bring these facts to bear upon the present political situation, and see how they affect it.

What does the present crisis in Armenia really mean ? Here is a race of sturdy peasants, the wealth producers of a not too prosperous Empire, threatened with extermination. For what reason ?

To say that the massacres are the results of an outbreak of religious fanaticism is, on the face of it, false. Everybody knows to-day that they were directly instigated by the Sultan ! Why ? Is he a criminal madman, wilfully slaughtering his most profitable subjects ? The astuteness of his policy shows that, if he is, he has at least many lucid intervals.

We must seek for the cause of these outrages not in Turkey, but in Russia ; there we shall find an answer.

As I have pointed out in a previous chapter, the emancipation of the serfs heralded a social revolution, and gave birth to political aspirations, which at present have no prospect of realisation. A school of thought sprang up in Russia, of which Nihilism was only a phase. This has infested dependent races, among which the Armenians are not the least intelligent. To combat these political aspirations, Russian statesmen have invented a strident nationalism, in which all political aims were to be merged, and all non-Russian races subject to the Tzar lost. But the Armenians could not contemplate with equanimity the extinction of their nationality, which, through centuries of persecution, had managed to preserve inviolate a religion, a culture, a language, and a literature which age has made respectable. We are therefore confronted by a great awakening of the Armenian race. It is damaging to the cause of the Armenians to represent them as miserable, helpless sheep. On the contrary, they have proved themselves lions. The records of Yildiz Kiosk may show what their resistance has cost the Sultan; but it is not likely that he will lower his prestige by publishing figures to prove how stubborn a stand they have made against his soldiery.

The Armenian national movement is of the greatest inconvenience to Russia, and if successful would throw all her calculations out of gear; an independent country between herself and Constantinople and Persia would be a thorn in her side.

Therefore the policy of extermination could only be grateful to Russia, and, in his endeavour to carry it out, the Sultan could count upon and has received her passive, if not her active, co-operation.

The course adopted by her Government in prohibiting my journey to Turkey across the frontiers of the Caucasus is an eloquent corroboration of this statement, if such were needed.

Russia's position as the protector of the confessors of the Orthodox religion has not suffered by this attitude, because the Armenian Christians do not belong to the Orthodox Church. In the case of Crete she was compelled to abandon her policy of friendship towards the Sultan.

Whether this national awakening of the Armenians. will prove successful or will turn out to be a death struggle remains to be seen ; but on March 12th, 1895, the *Daily Graphic* published the following sentences, which still express my opinions :—

"Much as cynics may sneer at it, what we call modern progress is an irresistible motive force which cannot to-day be dammed up for any length of time by any form of mediæval barbarism. In these days of rapid communications, of commercial enterprise, of newspapers and education, it is impossible to keep a people determined to join the great march of intellect out of the procession. Individual members will slip through the barriers of Governmental police, and get among the onward pressing throng. Their example will fire the rest, and no Kurds or Turks, nor even Russian Cossacks, will be able to keep them back.

What has happened in Armenia? Here and there Armenians have forced their way into the Universities of western Europe; numbers have emigrated to America. Is it possible that they could have been disinfected from all notions of liberty on their return? Their contagious ideas, on the contrary, have been transmitted throughout the length and breadth of their native land. Even the poor peasants of Sassun spoke to me of autonomy. And what force is Turkey opposing to this awakening? The disintegrating influence of uncivilised predatory nomadic tribes of Kurds. To them has been confided the salvation of Turkish Armenia. The situation is simply monstrous! Will these Kurds be able to dam up the swelling rivers of modern enlightenment which are showing signs already of broadening and overflowing their artificial banks? Assuredly not."

I do not believe that a national movement can be stopped, and I fancy that the Mrs. Partington mop of the Sultan is too feeble an instrument to stem the advancing tide.

Now Great Britain's duty is clear. If we allow the Sultan to continue uninterrupted in his present course of massacre and extermination he will not succeed— it is impossible to exterminate a nation in that way. But he will bring about a general disintegration of his dominions, and then the very thing that is feared will happen. The Powers will quarrel over the fragments. They are not ready for war at present, and they do not want this disintegration to occur until they are. That is the true inwardness of the situation.

In order to prevent this war, Great Britain should

step in before it is too late and restore order, by deposing the Sultan and granting an autonomy to Armenia ; not wait for the convenience of the Powers.

If we determine on adopting this course, we have two factors to consider : one is Turkey, the other the Powers.

Turkey, it is supposed, would oppose our passage of the Dardanelles. Let us grant that she would endeavour to do so. But what do we hear ? A Russian general has just inspected the Dardanelles, and has found them in so bad a condition that he has made a report urgently recommending changes and improvements.

Besides, it is doubtful whether the Turkish troops would make a very brave fight of it. They are as tired of the Sultan as most of his subjects, and many of the officers belong to the Young Turkey party.

We have been told that if we forced the Dardanelles we would run the risk of losing perhaps one or two of our battleships. That is an unpleasant contingency, but it is an argument which I hope would not deter our sailors from doing their duty. Besides, I am unsophisticated enough to believe that our battleships were built to fight as well as to be looked at.

The possible active interference of the Powers is another contingency. Let us review their position.

On paper, Russia is our most serious opponent, and perhaps our only active enemy in the present case. But, as I have shown in the previous chapter, the strength and efficiency of her navy are very much exaggerated, and she is so permeated with corruption that even a victorious war would be disastrous to her.

Within recent times Russia has had two European wars. The first, the Crimean, demonstrated to the satisfaction of everybody the collapse of the old *régime;* it was the death of Nicholas I., and it compelled Alexander II. to commence his reign with an era of reforms. The second, the Russo-Turkish war, was successful, but it revealed an amount of corruption in the Russian army which was simply appalling. The soldiers were fed on biscuits adulterated with plaster of Paris, while the generals drank champagne. The boots of the troops were made of paper. After the war an enquiry was held into the malversations of the authorities, with the result that three Grand Dukes, two of them commanders of armies, were banished, and several highly-placed persons imprisoned. That war, it is said, made such an impression upon Alexander III., then Heir Apparent, who also commanded an army, that his fanaticism for peace dates from that time. Besides, Russia is not prepared for, and cannot go to, war.

France is a more dangerous factor, but it is inconceivable that any Government could possibly face a war in favour of Turkey in view of the strong popular indignation against the Sultan. Countries like Austria, Germany, and France are nations under arms, and with the present state of feeling among the masses in Europe it is impossible for these countries to make war on any other pretext than that of self-defence. Unless they can raise the cry that the nation is in danger there is little probability of their being able to induce their subjects to bleed for them.

But I do not believe in the seriousness of the opposition of the Powers. That opposition is purely diplomatic, and simply intended to drive England into a corner and weaken her. It is the first step towards the settlement of the Egyptian question, which will be followed by the settlement of the South African question, and so on. The Powers may indeed unite to bring diplomatic pressure to bear upon us ; but I doubt whether they could so far sink their mutual differences as to effectually combine against us.

Diplomacy is like a game of chess, and everybody who plays the game by the recognised book openings knows exactly what moves must be made in certain circumstances. It is also very much like the art of war as followed by the polite and accomplished generals of Austria. Napoleon the Great, by his disregard for the old-fashioned rules of the game, drew down upon himself the condemnation of all polished soldiers, and was accused of ungentlemanly conduct ; but he won his battles. Prince Bismarck in the same way made use of the forms and rules of diplomacy in order to confound his opponents whenever he departed from them. Oliver Cromwell was not what we should call a diplomatist, but he knew how to uphold the dignity of England.

There is, however, another factor in international politics, besides diplomacy, which is perhaps even more important, and that is finance. The great financiers of Europe really pull the strings which make the puppets of politics dance. It is very generally believed that we are in Egypt to-day by the grace of the Egyptian bondholders. Since our occupation of that country those bonds have stood above par. The Turkish bonds are not at present an alluring investment, but it is quite possible that if we actively intervened in Turkey their financial status would be greatly improved. That consideration alone should carry weight with the bourses of Europe.

For all these reasons I am therefore of opinion that the Powers are playing a game of bluff. It is of course possible that we may have submitted a scheme for the partition of the Turkish Empire to which the Powers do not see their way to agree.

Unless this is the case, I do not think that anything can stand in the way of our actively intervening on behalf of Armenia. Should our Intelligence Branch opine that the Dardanelles were indeed impassable— which I do not think—why should we not land an expeditionary force at Alexandretta, and proceed to bombard the Turkish ports of the Levant? Cyprus still belongs to us.

There is an objection, and so far as I can see, only one, to our actively coercing the Sultan, and that is the probable impression such coercion might make on our Mahomedan subjects in India. That objection has been stated to me as a very valid one by an eminent British diplomatist. I do not think it amounts to much. From my experience of the Oriental mind, I am convinced that Orientals mistake consideration for weakness. We hold India by the sword, and unless we are able to keep it by the sword we shall lose it. Russia, who is herself only an Oriental country in disguise, understands these things better. A Russian officer explained to me one day that the celebrated Penjdeh incident owed its occurrence to the desire of the Russians to strike terror into the hearts of the Afghans. Orientals have been ruled by force so long that they understand no other argument than force.

Some people imagine that if we attempt to coerce Turkey, that would be the signal for a general massacre of the Christian European colony of Constantinople. But let it be clearly understood that if a Christian is killed the Sultan will be hanged like a common criminal, and I am convinced that not a hair of a Christian's head would be injured.

Then again it is objected, that even if an autonomy were granted to Armenia, that would not secure peace and order on account of the large Kurdish population, who would revolt.

From the depositions of the Sassun peasants and the lecture of Dr. Artzrun, I am inclined to think that is another bogy. There are Kurds and Kurds, and it would seem that some of them are even friendly towards the Armenians, while the Armenian peasants themselves told me that they stood in no fear of the Kurds, and that the massacres had not been perpetrated by them, but by Turkish troops. A *modus vivendi* could, I am confident, be found without difficulty between the Armenians and Kurds. We have seen that the Kurds actually made overtures to the Armenians to join forces with them against the Sultan. One of the most influential of the Kurds is a member of the Young Turkey party, and a violent enemy of the Sultan.

In the Caucasus we find the greatest harmony and good feeling existing between the Circassian, Georgian, Lisguin, and other native populations, and the Armenians, and there is consequently no reason to suppose that the same happy results could not be achieved in Turkish Armenia between the Armenians and the Kurds.

Before concluding I should like to say a few words about the dynamitards who entered the Ottoman Bank. These people have been reviled in the press as though they were common criminals. In the first place, it is not at all clear that they were not the creatures of *agents provocateurs*, for it is most incredible that the Sultan should have kept faith with them otherwise, seeing how frequently he has broken his word to his subjects. But supposing them to have been genuine Armenian revolutionaries, I am not so sure that the line of action they adopted was not patriotic. One thing at least must be admitted. They have, by their boldness and by provoking the massacres in Constantinople, brought the Armenian question a good many stages nearer towards solution. The selfishness of mankind is proverbial. While a hundred thousand or so of Armenians were killed in the obscure villages of Asia Minor nobody took more than a sort of academic interest in their fate; but as soon as Europe had these massacres brought to our very doors, as it were, and enacted in the full view of the Ambassadors of the Powers, the whole attitude of the world changed. America joined with England in the cry of indignation; even Germany, France, and Italy woke up. Everybody felt that things were getting serious.

When I was at Tiflis I was approached by several members of the violent revolutionary party and asked what in my opinion the effect of a whiff of dynamite would be on Europe in general. I implored them to discard all thoughts of dynamite outrages from their minds. By such measures, abhorrent to every civilised country, they would only alienate for ever the sympathy they then possessed. My very strong expression of disapproval seemed to convince them, and for over a year nothing was heard of dynamite.

But presumably their patience was exhausted. They had waited for the Powers to act, but the " Grandes Faiblesses " remained true to the nickname they have so righteously deserved, and meanwhile Armenians were being slaughtered by the hundred thousand. Is it surprising that they at last broke loose ? Rather should we wonder at their marvellous patience and moderation, and the diplomatic wisdom they displayed in taking possession of the Ottoman Bank and not blowing up Yildiz Kiosk, and thus provoking a general massacre of all the Christians.

Some of the enemies of the Armenians have described them to the European public as a lazy, scoundrelly set of rogues and thieves, who live by swindling the honest Mahomedan. That this is a gross and infamous libel I hope I have abundantly proved. Of course there are Armenian usurers, money-lenders, and blood-suckers, but I am given to understand that such persons may be found even in London and of the English race. Yet we would all of us be justly indignant if we were told that we were a nation of swindlers. The Armenian peasants are the wealth producers of Turkey—this cannot be too strongly insisted on ; and to give them their liberty could not have other than beneficial results for the entire civilised world. Nevertheless, abuse of the Armenians is no argument. Even if they were as vile as they are made out to be, that is only another reason why, in the interests of humanity at large, they should be liberated from conditions in which their moral nature has been warped, and be given a chance to work out their salvation.

England has to-day a great opportunity of re-asserting her ancient claim to be regarded as the friend of oppressed nationalities. And, fortunately for her, such action would be in accordance with her own best interests.

It is time that we showed the world that we are the descendants of the men who fought at Trafalgar, and that nearly a century of peace has not weakened our nerves or softened our muscles.

England is in great danger of being slowly but surely out-manœuvred and squeezed into a corner by the wily diplomatists of the Continent. Let us not wait for their convenience and until they are ready for us, but let us boldly take this Continental bull by the horns and be confident that God will defend the right.

If, however, it be decreed that we must go down, and that the great power and might of England's empire shall depart from us, then let us boldly "take it fighting," even as our British traditions would teach us to. Better to die like men than to fall to pieces like a decomposing corpse. It is not by weakly giving in to the Powers at every turn, as we have done of late, that this great Empire can be maintained. By the strength of our right arm have we won and made it, and by the strength of our right

U

arm must we keep and defend it against the jealous covetousness of our neighbours.

Therefore let every humane person, every patriotic Englishman, demand loudly the liberation of Armenia, and never think of the consequences. If we have to face a war let us face it, and remember that to-day the cause of the poor down-trodden Armenians is the cause of the British Empire.

THE END.

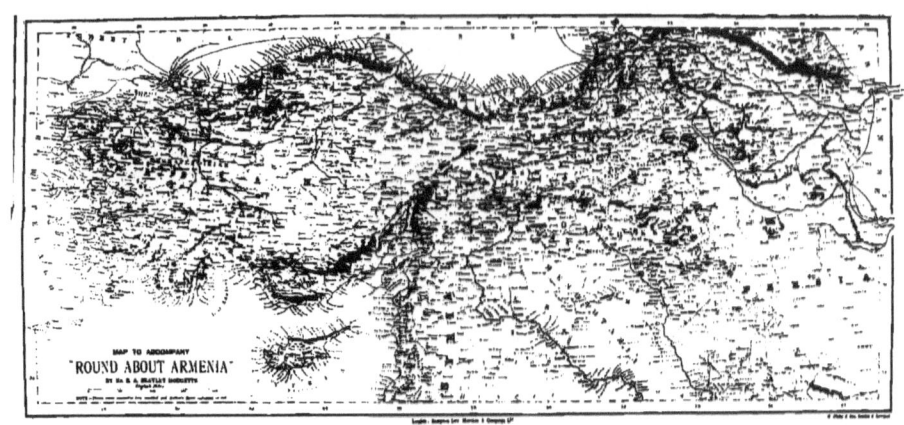

MAP TO ACCOMPANY
"ROUND ABOUT ARMENIA"
BY Mr. B. A. BRAYLEY HODGETTS
English Mile

INDEX.

ABUSES of Turkish régime, 27
Agricultural condition of Armenia, 118, 222, 243
Ahmid es Sultaneh, 186
——————————, I become his guest, 187
American missionaries in Trebizond, 39
Amusements of Cossack officers, 223
Andok, battle of, 96
Apology for Sultan, 18
Ardabil, 202
Aras, crossing the, 219
Armenia, extent of, 64
————, the Switzerland of the East, 266
Armenian amusements, 136
———— attitude towards Russia, 74, 240
———— ball, 144
———— brigands, 205
———— church, 65, 230
———— commercial travellers, 169
———— dinner-parties, 140
———— labour, annual emigratiou to Constantinople and Caucasus, 40
———— illusions about England, 104

Armenian ladies, elegance of, 145
———— merchants at Enzeli, 173
———— mercantile prosperity, decline of, 36
———— money-lender, 48
———— monks, 233, 238
———— national movement, inconvenience of, to Russia, 278
———— Question, the, 266
———— peasantry, their life, 40, 120
———— political parties in Tiflis, 62
————refugees, Russian Government instructions concerning, 59
———— schools at Etchmiadzin, 231, 241
———— soldiers, 79, 82
———— theatre, 16, 135
———— villages in the Caucasus, 222, 243
———— wedding, 142
———— women, industry of, 121
———— ————, state of education among, 138
Armenians and Russian Nihilists, 22, 75, 278
———— as American citizens, 22
———— compare favourably with the Dutch who revolted against Philip II., 110

Armenians, condition of, under Alexander II., 69, 72

——, condition of, under Alexander III., 73

—— in Constantinople, number of, 19

—— in Persia, comparative freedom of, 218

——, industry of, 109, 118, 126

—— of Tabreez, 212, 217

——, Russian opinion regarding them, 49, 83

——, the labourers of the East, 62, 109, 118, 126

Austrian commanding Russian steamer, 45

—— trade, 9

Astara, 198

BAKU, 147

Balakhanui, 163

Balaklava, 254

Bastinado, the, 178

Baths, Persian and Russian contrasted, 227

Batoum, 43, 245

—— Bibles, 210

Bismarck's policy towards England, 272

Bosphorus, 25

Bribery and the Sultan, 42

—— in Russia, examples of, 160

British Embassy at Constantinople, opinions of *attachés* regarding the massacres, 20

Buffer state between Russia, Turkey, and Persia, 267

Bulgaria, 3–11

Bulgarian army, 6

Byron's admiration for the Armenians, 109, 135

CAPITALISM of Europe, 275

Carpets, Persian, manufactured in England, 206

Cathedral of Etchmiadzin, 232

Catholicos, the, 66, 76, 235

Caspian, the, 167

Caucasus, industrial undertakings of, fatality about, 159

——, opinions of Russians concerning the, 49

——, police of the, 221

——, Russia's vulnerable point, 169, 221, 243, 247

—— scenery, 45

——, trade of, 84

Caviarre trade in Persia, 197

Character of Armenians vindicated, 288

Christian Missionaries and Mahomedans, 211

Chuppa travelling, 218

Circassians, 46

Colonies, 275

Condors, 206

Constantinople, 12

Continental hostility towards England, reason for, 272

Cossack Colonel, a typical, 247

Cotton growing in the Caucasus, 48

Cows of Armenia, 117

Crossing the mountains in Persia, 199

Culture of Armenians, 135

Curzon's view of Persia, 185

Cyprus, 284

DARDANELLES, 281, 284

Desolation of Sassun, 103

Despotisms of Russia, Turkey, and Persia compared, 178

Diligence drive through the Caucasus, 243

Diplomacy, 283
Dissatisfaction of commercial classes of Turkey, 35
Distrust amongst Armenians, 63, 81
Donkeys in Persia, their peculiarities, 206
Dreyfus and Co., 252
Dragomans, 17
Dynamitards, 286

EARLY marriages among Armenians, 139
Easter, 1895, how I spent it, 219
Egyptian Question, 283
Emigration of Mahomedans from Russia to Turkey, 153
England's danger, 289
——— duty, 269, 280
——— opportunity, 289
English and Russian Consuls, comparative position of, in the East, 30
——— and Russian soldiers in Afghanistan, 58
——— Consul of Resht, 183
——— ——— Tabreez, 208
——— ——— Trebizond, 28
——— journalist eludes police vigilance, 31
——— mechanics in the Turkish service, 17, 19
——— railway from Alexandretta to Tabreez, 217
Enzeli, 170
Erivan, 226
Etchmiadzin, 226

FAKIRS, 200, 204
Famine, the, of 1879 .. 123
Fanaticism and the massacres, 277
Fauna of Armenia, 116

Financiers of Europe and Turkish bonds, 284
Flora of Armenia, 115
Food in Persia, 193
France a dangerous factor, 282
French pioneer of industry in the Caucasus, 248

GEOGRAPHICAL position of England, 273
German views, 12
Germany and Russia, contrast between, 265
Gibbon's account of Armenia, 65
Governor-General of the Caucasus, 54
Grain trade of Russia, 251, 262
Greek merchants in Russia, 251, 261
Greeks discontented, 35

HAMEDJI, Turkish Cossacks, 34
Hardships of travelling in Persia, 205

IMPERIAL Bank of Persia, 186
Indifferent Armenians, 80
Industries of Armenians, 120
Insular angularity, 272
Isolation of England, 273

JEWISH merchants in southern Russia, 251, 261
Julfa, on the Russian frontier, 219

KERTCH, 252
Kerganarud, 194
Kourapatkine's, General, report, 184
Kurds, habitations of, 116
——— in the pay of Russia, 34
———, their treachery, 126

LAND tenure in Armenia, 127
Lawlessness in Turkey, illustration of this, 41
Legal status of Armenians in Turkey, 36
Library of Etchmiadzin, 233
Lobanoff-Rostovski, Prince, 3, 272

MACEDONIA, 9-11
Mahomedans in India, 285
Manna, 119
Massacres planned by Sultan, 37, 85
Mineral wealth of Armenia, 114
Modern progress and Armenia, 279
Molokane, 225
Moscow manufacturers, their influence and selfishness, 159
Mshakists, 74
Murghab, the, 175
Mrs. Partington and the Sultan, 280
Museum of the Caucasus, 53

NAVAL officers, life of, at Sevastopol, 256
New Athens, 249
Nihilism, 278
Nicholas II., his famous speech, 148
Nobel syndicate, 157
Novorossisk, 251

ODESSA, 260
Oil industry of Baku, 156
————, selfish policy of Government towards, 158
Origin of Sassun massacres, 90, 277

PARK of Baku, 155
Passport difficulties, 31, 56, 173, 214, 227, 242

Pasturages of Armenia, 117
Pera, 16
Persia a Russian protectorate, 186
———, arrival in, 170
———, decay of, 206
———, English influence in, on the wane, 185
———, enterprise in, Russia's opposition to all, 186
Persia's policy, views of a Persian statesman, 187
Persian bazaars, 181, 208
——— bits, 195
——— boatmen, 172
——— bulls, 175
——— cavalry, 193, 194
——— Consul-General of Tiflis, 56
——— costumes, 181
——— frontier, anarchy there, 211
——— flag prohibited on the Caspian, 171
——— Government, 178
——— Gulf, Russia wants to get there, 185, 267
——— horses, 193
——— hospitality, my experience of, 190
——— peasantry, 177
——— subjects of Russia prefer Russian rule, 198
——— women, 182
Persians, compared with Turks, 181
Piano-tuners in the East, 241
Pir Bazaar, 174
—. ———, Armenian clerks at, 174
—. ——— road to Resht, 176
Pit of Galeguzan, 97, 100, 107
Policy of England, 273
Polygamy, 12
Popular feeling on the Continent would prevent war, 282

Ports of Black Sea, Turkish, 26
Powers bluffing, 283
——, conspiracy of the, against England, 271
Printing works of Etchmiadzin, 241
Protection, 275
Punishments inflicted by Turks on Armenians, 101

RESHT, 180
Revolutionary Armenian party, 79, 287
Rothschild Oil Syndicate, 157
Rouble, the rise of the, 263
Russia and Turkey, 73, 279
——, cause of Armenian outrages to be sought in, 277
——, England's most serious opponent, 281
Russian ambitions, 267
—— Black Sea fleet, 255, 259
—— colonies on the Caspian, 197
—— Consul of Resht, 184
—— —— Tabreez, 208
—— —— Trebizond, 33
—— custom-house officials, 220
—— Government prohibits my travelling in the Caucasus, 55
—— influence at Resht, 175
—— merchants, debauched life of, 164
—— middle-classes, their attitude towards the Government, 244, 253
—— monks, 250, 265
—— Navy, 258
—— officers at Tiflis, 58
—— peasants, 197, 264
—— population of the Caucasus, 83

Russian public schools and the Armenians, 84
—— railway schemes for Persia, 184
—— sects, exiled to the Caucasus, 225
Russia's altered attitude towards Armenia, 71, 231
—— hold on Persian trade, 185
—— political condition, 69, 278
—— power of concentrating troops for a descent on India or Persia, 168
—— renascence, 67

SASSUN massacres, story of, 85
Sentimental enthusiasm of the British public, 268
Sevan, the Siberia of Armenian monks, 243
Sevastopol, 255
Shah's palace at Enzeli, 171
Sheep of Armenia, 117
Silk culture, Russian Government fostering, 48
Sofia, 5
Socialism, causes of, 275
——, fear of, on the Continent, 276
Sourakhani, 164
South African Question, 283
Stambuloff, 8
——, a believer in a great Slavonic Republic, 75
Steamers on the Caspian, 167, 169
Stoiloff, 8
Sulphur Baths of Tiflis, 54
Sultan, character of, 14
——, passion for detail of, 19
Sweating at Baku, 157
—— in Persia, 172

TABREEZ, 208, 216
Tarantass travelling, 221
Tartar millionaires at Baku, 164
Taxation of Armenians in Turkey, 127, 130
Tea-growing in the Caucasus, 46
Terrell, Mr., interview with, 21
Theatrical enterprises, cost of, in Russia, 165
Tiflis, 51
Timber, scarcity of, 115
Tobacco-fields of Enzeli, 175
Top-hané, 16
Trebizond, 28
————, life at, 33
Turk, laziness of, 127
Turkish Consul of Tabreez, 214
———— fleet, 14
———— misrule in Asia Minor, 26
———— peasantry, condition of, 27
———— spies on my track, 56, 170, 181, 189, 213

Turkish troops, 20, 26, 29
———— tired of Sultan, 281
———— uniforms, evidences of Russian influence, 19

UNITED STATES, opinions of American Minister, 21

VALI of Trebizond, 32
Vices of Armenians, 122
Villages destroyed at Sassun, list of, 111

WAR, danger of, 280
——, England to prevent, 280
——, Russia's dread of, 282
Washing in Persia, 193
Wines of Armenia, 119

YOUNG Turkey Party, 12

ZEKKI PASHA, 16, 18

LONDON: PRINTED BY WILLIAM CLOWES AND SONS, LIMITED.
STAMFORD STREET AND CHARING CROSS.